The Plutarch Project

Volume Six

Aemilius Paulus, Aristides, and Solon

by

Anne E. White

CONTENTS

Introduction..i

Aemilius Paulus 1

Lesson One 4

Lesson Two 8

Lesson Three 13

Lesson Four 17

Lesson Five 22

Lesson Six 26

Lesson Seven 30

Lesson Eight 34

Lesson Nine 39

Lesson Ten...44

Lesson Eleven..49

Lesson Twelve and Examination Questions 53

Aristides 59

Lesson One 61

Lesson Two 64

Lesson Three 68

Lesson Four 73

Lesson Five 77

Lesson Six 82

Lesson Seven 86

Lesson Eight 91

Lesson Nine 95

Lesson Ten 99

Lesson Eleven 103

Lesson Twelve and Examination Questions 108

Solon 113

Lesson One 114

Lesson Two 118

Lesson Three 121

Lesson Four 125

Lesson Five 130

Lesson Six 133

Lesson Seven 137

Lesson Eight 140

Lesson Nine 143

Lesson Ten 145

Lesson Eleven 151

Lesson Twelve and Examination Questions 154

Bibliography 158

Introduction

These notes, and the accompanying text, are prepared for the use of individual students and small groups following a twelve-week term. The text is that of Thomas North's 1579 translation of Plutarch's *Lives of the Noble Greeks and Romans*, with substitutions from John Dryden's 1683 translation [in brackets]. I have updated spelling and punctuation. Omissions for length and/or suitability are noted.

Using the Lesson Material

Each study contains explanatory material before the first lesson. A little at the beginning may be useful to stir interest in the study, but it is not meant to be given all in one dose!

Some lessons are divided into two or three sections. These can be read all at once or used throughout the week.

I encourage you to make the lessons your own. Use the questions that are the most meaningful to you. Remember that Charlotte Mason was satisfied with "Proper names are written on the blackboard, and then the children narrate what they have listened to."

Examination Questions

The three studies include suggestions for end-of-term examinations. The questions for this volume were drawn from original P.N.E.U. programmes.

The Plutarch Project

Aemilius Paulus

(229-160 B.C.)

"When I first began to write these lines, my intent was to profit other[s]: but since, continuing and going on, I have much profited myself by looking into these histories, as if I looked into a glass, to frame and fashion my life to the mould and pattern of these virtuous noblemen." —Plutarch

Who was Aemilius?

Lucius Æmilius Paulus Macedonicus was usually called Aemilius or Aemilius Paulus. He was a Roman statesman, consul, and general during the Third Macedonian War, which lasted from 171 to 168 B.C., and which makes up a large part of the story. However, Aemilius had a long career in Roman government before his election as **consul** and his accompanying duties as military general. The first few lessons follow him through his positions as **aedile**, **praetor** (with special honours), and **consul** (twice). He had a second, separate position as an **augur**, an omen-reading priest. Plutarch says that Aemilius took the job of being an augur so seriously that he raised it to an art form.

He also took his role as military commander very seriously. Plutarch finds it noteworthy that he personally taught (instructed, coached) the soldiers under his command. We get a picture already of an extraordinary man; perhaps one who made an art form of "being a Roman."

The spelling of Aemilius Paulus

In many printed or typed texts where it's difficult to reproduce an Æ, you will see it spelled just AE— or Ae—, so I have used that form. In online searches, you might also try reversing the names, i.e. Paulus Aemilius. Paulus is occasionally spelled Paullus.

What is the commonwealth?

The phrase translated "commonwealth" comes from the Latin "Res publica," that which is held in common (and the root of the word "republic"). More generally, it refers to the state itself, the Roman Republic. "Matters of commonwealth," for Aemilius and his colleagues, would be state duties.

The rankings of civil leaders in Rome

From top to bottom, the governing officials were **dictator** (a position filled only during times of crisis), **consul**, **praetor**, **aedile**, and **quaestor**. There were more than one of each at a time—two consuls, eight praetors, and so on. The rank of **censor** could be given to ex-consuls. There were also **tribunes**, but they were drawn from a different social class than the others.

People in this Story

Family and Friends of Aemilius

Scipio and **Fabius Maximus (1):** sons of Aemilius. The first was properly named Publius Cornelius Scipio Africanus Aemilianus; he became the hero of the Third Punic War. The second was Quintus Fabius Maximus Aemilianus, who was later a consul. Following

Aemilius' divorce from their mother, his remarriage to a second wife, and the birth of two more sons (and at least one daughter), the boys were adopted into other noble families (see below).

Fabius Maximus (2): Quintus Fabius Maximus Rullianus, the adoptive father of Aemilius' eldest son. He was the grandson or great-grandson of Quintus Fabius Maximus Verrucosus (280-203 B.C.), who was the subject of Plutarch's *Life of Fabius.*

Scipio Africanus: The first Roman by this name was **Scipio Africanus the Elder**, or Publius Cornelius Scipio Africanus (236-183 B.C.); he was a hero of the Second Punic War, which earned him the name "Africanus." He married the sister of Aemilius Paulus, **Aemilia**. It was his son **Scipio Africanus the Younger** who, not having an heir of his own, adopted his nephew, the second son of Aemilius, who also became known as **Scipio.**

Aelius Tubero: a son-in-law of Aemilius

Rulers of Macedon

Philip V, who officially became king in 229 B.C. at the age of nine, and who reigned independently from 221-179 B.C.; he was the son of **Demetrius II Aetolicus**, and the father of **Perseus.**

Top Ten Terms in *Aemilius Paulus*

If you recognize these words, you're well on your way to mastering North's vocabulary. (They will not be noted in the lessons.)

1. **Acquaint:** To **acquaint** is used several times, meaning either "to become used to, familiar with" or "to share information."

2. **Divers:** several

3. **Footmen:** foot soldiers

4. **Spoil** or **spoils:** items seized from an enemy; loot

5. **Stay:** delay, detain, stop

6. **Strait:** tight, narrow. To be **strait** with people means to be restrictive or stingy. A **strait** is a narrow channel of water.

7. **Strange:** usually means "foreign," but sometimes just means "strange." Soldiers that are **strangers** are often foreign mercenaries (working for any army that will pay them).

8. **Sundry:** various

9. **Target:** shield

10. **Voward:** front. Soldiers in the **voward** are those leading the troops. The **voward of his battle** means the front of his troops.

    Bonus phrase: "**The barbarous people**" or **barbarians** usually refers to the **Persians**, who are sometimes called the **Medes**. In one place it means the Lusitanians.

Lesson One

Introduction

Plutarch begins this *Life* with some family background. The first Aemilius was given his name because of "the sweetness and pleasant grace of his tongue." The word "aemulus" is the root of our word "emulation," which means striving to do well, often with a sense of trying both to imitate or match and then to outperform others. (The names Amelia and Emily are English derivatives.) Name books also use the word "industrious" or "eager," and you will see that Plutarch's subject Aemilius Paulus was both.

> "If we are learning to skate, we have no peace till we
> skate as well as a boy we know who learned last
> winter; then we want to outdo him; then, to skate as
> well as another better skater; then, to outdo him;
> and so on, and when we go to bed at night we dream
> of the day when we shall skate better than anyone in
> the neighbourhood; nay, we think how glorious it
> would be to be the very best skater in the whole
> world." (Charlotte Mason, *Ourselves*)

Vocabulary

ancient and patrician houses: oldest and noblest families

the first of the house…: the first ancestor named Aemilius

surnamed: given the additional honourary name

consul, aedile, augur: see introductory notes

fawning: trying to win favour by insincere flattery

sued for: ran for

contending: arguing, getting into conflict

negligence: neglect of duty. To **give a precedent for remissness** is to open the door to **negligence.**

commonwealth: see introductory note

notorious breach of its laws: great criminal act

trifles: small things

ingratiate himself: make himself popular

contemned: treated with contempt; scorned

People

Lucius Paulus: the father of Aemilius Paulus, twice elected consul

Scipio the Great: Scipio Africanus the Elder; see introductory notes

Historic Occasions

229 B.C.: birth of Aemilius Paulus

218 B.C.: Second Punic War

216 B.C.: The **Battle of Cannae** against the Carthaginians, where the Romans were badly defeated and Aemilius' father was killed

212 B.C.: birth of Perseus of Macedon

200 B.C.: Second Macedonian War

193 B.C.: Aemilius became aedile

On the Map

A map showing the Roman Republic during this period (the time just before the conquest of Greece) would be helpful.

Reading

Prologue

[Almost all historians agree that the Aemilii were one of the **ancient and patrician houses** in Rome.] Some writers affirm also that **the first of the house that gave name to all the posterity after**, was Marcus [Dryden: *Mamercus*], the son of Pythagoras the Wise, **surnamed** Aemilius for the sweetness and pleasant grace of his tongue. [Most of this race that have risen through their merit to reputation also enjoyed good fortune; and even the misfortune to **Lucius Paulus** at the **Battle of Cannae** gave testimony to his wisdom and valour.] For he [Lucius Paulus] was forced to fight against his will, when he saw he could not bridle the rashness of his fellow **consul** that [insisted on engaging in] battle, and to do as [the other consul] did; [on the contrary, when he that was so resolute to engage deserted him in the midst of danger, he kept the field] and fought it valiantly unto the last gasp.

This Aemilius left a daughter behind him called Aemilia, which was married unto **Scipio the Great**; and a son, Aemilius Paulus, being the same man whose life we presently treat of.

Part One

His youth fortunately fell out in a flourishing time of glory and honour, through the sundry virtues of many great and noble persons living in those days, among whom he made his name famous also: and it was not by that ordinary art and course which the best esteemed young men of that age did take and follow. For he did not use to plead private men's causes in law, neither would creep into men's favour by **fawning** upon any of them: though he saw it a common practice, and policy of men, to seek the people's favour and good wills by such means. [Not that he was incapable of either, but he chose to purchase a much more lasting glory by his valour, justice, and integrity, and in these virtues he soon outstripped all his equals.]

The first office of honour he **sued for** was the office of **aedile**, in which suit he was preferred before twelve other[s] that sued for the selfsame office: who were men of no small quality, for they all came afterwards to be consuls. After this, he was chosen to be one of the number of the priests whom the Romans call **augurs**: who have the charge of all the divinations and soothsayings, in telling of things to come by flying of birds, and signs in the air. He was so careful, and took such pains to understand how the Romans did use the same, and with such diligence sought the observation of the ancient religion of Romans in all holy matters: that where that priesthood was before esteemed but a title of honour, and desired for the name only: he brought it to pass that it was the most honourable science, and best reputed of in Rome. Wherein he confirmed the philosophers' opinion that religion is [the science of worshipping the gods]. For when he did anything belonging to his office of priesthood, he did it with great experience, judgment, and diligence, leaving all other thoughts, and without omitting any ancient ceremony, or adding to any new, **contending** oftentimes with his companions, in things which seemed light, and of small moment: declaring unto them, that though we do presume the gods are easy to be pacified, and that they readily pardon all faults and scapes committed by **negligence;** [yet any such laxity was a very dangerous thing for a **commonwealth** to allow; because no man ever began the disturbance of his country's peace by a **notorious breach of its laws**; and those who are careless in **trifles give a precedent for remissness** in important duties. Nor was he less severe in requiring and observing the ancient Roman discipline in military affairs; not endeavouring, where he had the command, to **ingratiate himself** with his soldiers by popular flattery, though this custom prevailed at that time.]

[short omission]

But [he] himself did, [in an orderly way], show them the very rules and precepts of the discipline of wars, even as a priest that should express the names and ceremonies of some holy sacrifice wherein were danger to omit any part or parcel. [And by severity to such as transgressed and **contemned** those laws, he maintained his country in its former greatness, esteeming victory over enemies itself but as an accessory to the proper training and disciplining of the citizens.]

Narration and Discussion

How was Aemilius different from other young men of his time?

Aemilius said that "to overcome the enemy by force was but an accessory, as a man may term it, in respect of well training and ordering his citizens by good discipline" (North's translation). How was this an unusual belief for a Roman commander?

For older students: Aemilius raised the position of augur to a high art or science. Christians are commanded to have nothing to do with such divination. Can you explain (nevertheless) what positive aspects this story shows of his character?

Lesson Two

Introduction

Plutarch continues the introduction to Aemilius, including his marriages, children, and the events leading up to the war against Perseus.

Vocabulary

against Antiochus the Great: see **Historic Occasions** note for **Lesson Three**

up in arms in Spain: there was ongoing revolt by the **Lusitanians,** a tribe living in what is now western Spain and Portugal

praetor, consul: see introductory notes

axes: symbols of Roman power and authority

fealty: loyalty

drachma: a silver coin

but remiss in: not very good at

answer his wife's dowry: on the death of a husband, the widow's dowry was paid back to her

had triumphed: had been publicly recognized for a military victory

trafficked: bought or sold goods

onset: attack

rampart or bulwark: protection

razed only the fortifications: destroyed only their military posts or barricades, not the towns themselves

a little more curiously: a little more notably

People

Scipio and **Fabius Maximus (1), Fabius Maximus (2), Scipio Africanus, Aelius Tubero:** see introductory notes

son of Cato: see **Lesson Seven**

Ligurians: explained in the text

Historic Occasions

191 B.C.: Aemilius became praetor

191-189 B.C.: Aemilius sent against the **Lusitanians** (in **Part One**)

182 B.C.: Aemilius elected consul (first term)

181 B.C.: Aemilius sent against the **Ligurians** (in **Part Two**)

On the Map

A map of the Roman Republic will again be useful.

Reading

Part One

While the Romans were in wars **against Antiochus the Great**, in the south parts, all the chiefest captains of Rome being employed [*in that way*]; [there arose another war in the west, and they were all **up in arms in Spain.**] Thither they sent Aemilius [as] **praetor**, not with six axes as the other praetors had borne before them, but with twelve: so that under the name of praetor, he had the authority and dignity of a **consul.** He twice overcame the barbarous people in battle, and slew thirty thousand of them, and got this victory through his great skill and wisdom in choosing the advantage of place and time to fight with his enemies, even as they passed over a river: which easily gave his soldiers the victory.

Moreover, he took there two hundred and fifty cities, all which did open and gladly receive him in. So, leaving that country quiet and in good peace, and having received their **fealty** by oath made between his hands, he returned again to Rome, not enriched [by] the value of a **drachma** more than before. [And, indeed, he was **but remiss in** making money; though he always lived freely and generously on what he had, which was so far from being excessive, that after his death there was barely enough to **answer his wife's dowry.**]

His first wife was Papiria, [the daughter of Maso, who had formerly been consul]. After they had lived a long time together, he was divorced from her, notwithstanding he had goodly children by her. For by her he had that famous **Scipio** and **Fabius Maximus (1).**

[omission about common marital woes, and the causes of Aemilius' divorce]

So Aemilius, having put away Papiria his first wife, he married another that brought him two sons, which he brought up with himself in his house; and [he] gave his two first sons in adoption to two of the noblest and richest families of the city of Rome. [The elder was adopted into the house of **Fabius Maximus (2)** who was five times consul; the younger by the son of Scipio Africanus, his cousin, and was by him named Scipio.]

Concerning his daughters, the **son of Cato** married the one, and **Aelius Tubero** the other, who was a marvellous honest man, and did more nobly maintain himself in his poverty than any other Roman: for they were sixteen persons all of one name, and of the house of the Aelians, very near kin one to the other, who had all but one little house in the city, and a small farm in the country, wherewith they entertained themselves, and lived all together in one house, with their wives and many little children. Amongst their wives, one of them was the daughter of Aemilius Paulus (after he had been twice consul, and **had triumphed** twice), not being ashamed of her husband's poverty, but wondering at his virtue that made him poor.

[*omission about family life*]

Part Two

Now Aemilius, being chosen **consul**, went to make war with the **Ligurians**. These are very valiant and warlike men, and were very good soldiers at that time, by reason of their continual wars against the Romans, whose near neighbours they were. For they dwelt in the furthest part of Italy, that bordereth upon the great Alps, and the row of Alps, whereof the foot joineth to the Tuscan Sea, and pointeth towards Africa, and are mingled with the Gauls, and Spaniards, neighbours unto that seacoast: who, scouring all the Mediterranean Sea at that time unto Hercules' Pillars, [in light vessels fitted for that purpose, robbed and destroyed all that **trafficked** in those parts].

Aemilius being gone to seek them in their country, they tarried his coming with an army of forty thousand men; nevertheless, though he had but eight thousand men in all, and that they were five to one of his, yet he gave the **onset** upon them, and overthrew them, and drove them into their cities. Then he sent to offer them peace, for the Romans would not altogether destroy the Ligurians, because their country was a **rampart or bulwark** against the invasion of the Gauls, who lay lurking for opportunity and occasion to invade Italy: whereupon these Ligurians yielded themselves unto him and put all their forts and ships into his hands.

[He, at the utmost, **razed only the fortifications** and delivered their towns to them again; but took away all their shipping with him, leaving them no vessels bigger than those of three oars; and set at liberty great numbers of prisoners they had taken both by sea and land, strangers as well as Romans. These were the acts most worthy of remark in his first consulship.]

Part Three

Afterwards, he oftentimes showed himself very desirous to be consul again, and did put forth himself to sue for it: but when he was denied it, he never after made suit for it again, but gave himself only to study divine things, and to see his children virtuously brought up, not only in the Roman tongue which himself was taught, but also, **a little more curiously**, in the Greek tongue. [To this purpose he not only procured masters to teach them grammar, logic, and rhetoric, but had for them also preceptors in modelling and drawing, managers of horses and dogs, and instructors in field sports, all from Greece.] And he himself also (if no matters of commonwealth troubled him) was ever with them in the school when they were at their books; and also when they otherwise did exercise themselves. For he loved his children as much, or more, than any other Roman.

Narration and Discussion

What were the most noteworthy acts in Aemilius' first consulship? How did he react when he was passed over for a second consulship?

Describe the educational curriculum of the children of Aemilius. Was it anything like yours?

Creative narration: You are a reporter sent to the house of Aemilius to interview him about wars and political matters. However, the interview is sidetracked by family activities. Write or act out the scene.

Lesson Three

Introduction

In this lesson, we meet Perseus of Macedon, who was called "mean" and "sordid." It is said that he lacked courage, and that he was noted for his covetous character. It was even rumored that he might have been the son of a seamstress and not a true prince at all. However, he was a good military commander, and he used what his father Philip had stored up to gain an early advantage over the Romans.

Vocabulary

preferred: proposed

husband: manager, steward

near unto the city of Scotusa: this refers to the **Battle of Cynoscephalae** (see note below)

escaped good cheap: got off lightly

coming to understand himself: thinking it over again

disdain: resent

to the end: with the purpose

corn: grain

entertain ten thousand strangers in pay: pay ten thousand mercenary (foreign) soldiers

spurious: questionable

Historic Occasions

202 B.C.: Roman defeat of **Hannibal** at the Battle of Zama

197 B.C.: Roman defeat of **Philip V of Macedon** at the Battle of Cynoscephalae (referred to here as **Scotusa**)

192 B.C.: Roman defeat of **Antiochus III "the Great,"** ruler of the
Seleucid Empire, at the Battle of Magnesia

179 B.C.: Perseus became king of Macedon after the death of his father

On the Map

To the regions already mentioned (the Roman Republic; the Greek
states including Macedon), you might add **Carthage**.

Reading

Part One

Now concerning the state of the commonwealth, the Romans were at
wars with **King Perseus**, and they much blamed the captains they had
sent thither before; for that for lack of skill and courage, they had so
cowardly behaved themselves, as their enemies laughed them to scorn;
[and they did less hurt to the enemy than they received from him].

For not long before, they had driven **King Antiochus** beyond
Mount Taurus, and had made him forsake the rest of Asia, and had
shut him up within the borders of Syria: who was glad that he had
bought that country with fifteen thousand talents, which he paid for a
fine. A little before also, they had overcome **Philip, King of
Macedon**, in Thessaly, and had delivered the Greeks from the
bondage of the Macedonians. And moreover, having overcome
Hannibal (unto whom no prince nor king that ever was in the world
was comparable, either for his power or valiantness) they thought this
too great a dishonour to them, that this war they had against King
Perseus should hold so long of even hand with them, as if he had been
an enemy equal with the people of Rome: considering also that they
fought not against them, but with the refuse and scattered people of
the overthrown army his father had lost before; and [they understood]
not that Philip had left his army stronger, and more expert by reason
of his overthrow, than it was before.

*[omission for length: details of the Macedonian rulers just before Perseus, ending
with Philip, his father]*

Philip in his green youth gave more hope of himself, than any other of the kings before: insomuch they thought that one day he would restore Macedon her ancient fame and glory, and that he alone would pluck down the pride and power of the Romans, who rose against all the world. But after that [he] had lost a great battle and was overthrown by Titus Quinctius Flaminius **near unto the city of Scotusa**: then he began to quake for fear, and to leave all to the mercy of the Romans, thinking he **escaped good cheap** for any light ransom or tribute the Romans should impose upon him. Yet afterwards **coming to understand himself**, he grew to **disdain** it much, thinking that to reign through the favour of the Romans was but to make himself a slave, to seek to live in pleasure at his ease, and not for a valiant and noble prince born. Whereupon he set all his mind to study the discipline of wars; and [he] made his preparations as wisely and closely as possibly he could.

For he left all his towns alongst the seacoast, and standing upon any highways, without any fortification at all, and in manner desolate without people, **to the end** [that] there might appear no occasion of doubt or mistrust in him: and in the meantime, in the high countries of his realm, far from great beaten ways, he levied a great number of men of war, and replenished his towns and strongholds that lay scatteringly abroad, with armour and weapon[s], money, and men, providing for war, which he kept as secretly as he could. For he had provision of armour in his armoury to arm thirty thousand men; [he had] eight million bushels of **corn** safely locked up in his forts and strong places; and [he had] ready money, as much as would serve to **entertain ten thousand strangers in pay**, to defend his country for the space of ten years. But before he could bring that to pass he had purposed, he died for grief and sorrow; after he knew he had unjustly put **Demetrius**, the best of his sons, to death, upon the false accusation of the worst, that was **Perseus**.

Part Two

As [Perseus] did inherit the kingdom of his father by succession, so did he also inherit his father's malice against the Romans. But he had no shoulders to bear so heavy a burden, and especially being as he was, a man of so vile and wicked nature: for among many [faults and diseases of various sorts, covetousness bore the chief place. There is a statement also of his not being true-born; that the wife of King Philip took him from his mother, Gnathaenion (a woman of Argos, that earned her living as a seamstress), as soon as he was born, and passed him upon her husband as her own. And this might be the chief cause of his contriving the death of [his brother] Demetrius; as he might well fear that, so long as there was a lawful successor in the family, there was not security that his **spurious** birth might not be revealed.]

Notwithstanding, simple though [Perseus] was, and of [so] vile and base [a] nature, he found the strength of his kingdom so great that he was contented to take [it] upon him to make war against the Romans, which he maintained a long time; and fought against their consuls that were their generals, and repulsed great armies of theirs both by sea and land; and overcame some [of them].

[He routed Publius Licinius, who was the first that invaded Macedonia, in a cavalry battle; slew twenty-five hundred practiced soldiers, and took six hundred prisoners; and surprising their fleet as they rode at anchor before Orens, he took twenty ships of burden with all their lading, sunk the rest that were freighted with **corn**, and, besides this, made himself master of four galleys with five banks of oars. He fought a second battle with Hostilius, a consular officer, as he was making his way into the country at Elimiae, and forced him to retreat; and, when he afterwards by stealth designed an invasion through Thessaly, challenged him to fight, which the other feared to accept.]

Narration and Discussion

What was Philip's strategy against the Romans? Might he have been successful if he had lived longer?

Why was Perseus so successful in his first attempts to defend his kingdom?

For older students: how does Plutarch distinguish "covetousness" from the more honourable "emulation?"

Lesson Four

Introduction

Imagine two cameras focused on our main characters. Aemilius Paulus, at the age of almost sixty, was unanimously chosen as consul for a second term, because Rome was in desperate need of a general who would act like a general. When he told the Romans that he required absolute power and total command, they quickly agreed: they had nothing to lose and everything to gain.

Perseus, on the other hand, doubted his own authority, and began to lose control.

Vocabulary

Bastarnae: a tribe living between the Carpathian Mountains and the Dnieper River. Plutarch also calls them "the **Gauls.**"

by favour or solicitation: Leaders had previously been those who more or less chose themselves; but it was now time to be more deliberate and strategic.

importune: beg

the marketplace: the Forum in Rome

which province should fall to his share: High officials each had the additional responsibility of a territory outside of Rome.

that sued for the charge: that had run for the consulship

happy issue: positive outcome

peradventure: perhaps

grazing: farming livestock

this barbarous supply: these mercenary soldiers

damped: dejected

steward: A steward is a manager, often quite important; but the point here is that Perseus was acting as if he were accountable to the Romans rather than to his own people.

husbanded and preserved: taken care of, saved

manifest: clear

Historic Occasions

171 B.C.: Beginning of the Third Macedonian War; **Gentius of Illyria** allied his kingdom with the Romans

169 B.C.: Gentius changed sides to support the Macedonians

168 B.C.: Aemilius elected consul (second term)

Reading

Prologue

Furthermore, as though the war troubled [Perseus] nothing at all, and that he had cared little for the Romans: he went and fought a battle in the meantime with the Dardanians, where he slew ten thousand of those barbarous people, and brought a marvellous great spoil away with him. Moreover, he procured the nation of the **Gauls** (also called **Bastarnae**), dwelling upon the River Danube: men very warlike, and excellent good horsemen. He did practise with the Illyrians also by mean[s] of their **King Gentius**, to make them join with him in these wars.

[short omission for length]

Part One

[The Romans, being advertised of these things, thought it necessary no longer to choose their commanders **by favour or solicitation**; but of their own motion to select a general of wisdom and capacity for the management of great affairs. And such was Aemilius Paulus, advanced in years, being nearly [sixty], yet vigorous in his own person, and rich in valiant sons and sons-in-law, besides [having] a great number of influential relations and friends, all of whom joined in urging him to yield to the desires of the people, who called him to the consulship.]

At the beginning, indeed he delayed the people much that came to **importune** him, and utterly denied them: saying he was no meet man neither to desire, nor yet to take upon him any charge. Howbeit in the end, seeing the people did urge it upon him, by knocking continually at his gates, and calling him aloud in the streets, willing him to come into **the marketplace**; and perceiving they were angry with him because he refused it, he was content to be persuaded.

And when he stood among them that sued for the consulship, the people thought straight that he stood not there so much for desire of the office, as for that he put them in hope of assured victory, and happy success of this begun war: so great was their love towards him, and the good hope they had of him, that they chose him consul again the second time. [Nor would they suffer the lots to be cast, as was usual, to determine **which province should fall to his share**; but immediately decreed him the command of the Macedonian war.]

[*brief omission*]

The Romans had a custom at that time, that such as were elected consuls (after that they were openly proclaimed) should make an oration of thanks unto the people, for the honour and favour they had showed him. The people then (according to the custom) being gathered together to hear Aemilius speak, he made this oration unto them:

> That the first time he sued to be consul, was in
> respect of himself, standing at that time in need of
> such honour: [but] now he offered himself the
> second time unto it, for the good love he bare unto
> them who stood in need of a general, [upon which
> account he thought there was no thanks due]. And if
> they did think also this war might be better followed
> by any other than by himself, he would presently
> with all his heart resign the place. Furthermore, if
> they had any trust or confidence in him, that they

thought him a man sufficient to discharge it: then
that they would not speak nor meddle in any matter
that concerned his duty, and the office of a general;
saving only, that they would be diligent (without
any words) to do whatsoever he commanded, and
should be necessary for the war and service they
took in hand. [For if they proposed to command
their own commander, they would render this
expedition more ridiculous than the former.]

These words made the Romans very obedient to him, and [they] conceived good hope to come, being all of them very glad that they had refused those ambitious flatterers **that sued for the charge**, and [that they] had given it unto a man that [dared] boldly and frankly tell them the truth. [So entirely did the people of Rome, that they might rule, and become masters of the world, yield obedience and service to reason and superior virtue.]

Part Two

[That Aemilius, setting forward to the war, by a prosperous voyage and successful journey, arrived with speed and safety at his camp I attribute to good Fortune; but, when I see how the war under his command was brought to a **happy issue**, partly by his own daring boldness, partly by his good counsel, partly by the ready administration of his friends, partly by his presence of mind and skill to embrace the most proper advice in the extremity of danger, I cannot ascribe any of his remarkable and famous actions (as I can those of other commanders) to his so much celebrated good Fortune.)] Unless you will say, **peradventure**, that Perseus' covetousness and misery was Aemilius' good fortune: for his miserable fear of spending money was the only cause and destruction of the whole realm of Macedon, which was in good state and hope of continuing in prosperity.

[The following events took place before Aemilius' arrival]

For there came down into the country of Macedon, at King Perseus' request, ten thousand **Bastarnae** a-horseback, and as many footmen to them, who always joined with them in battle, all mercenary soldiers, depending upon pay and entertainment of wars. [These were men] that could not plow nor sow, nor traffic merchandise by sea, nor [had] skill of **grazing** to gain their living with; and to be short, that had no other occupation or merchandise but to serve in the wars, and to overcome those with whom they fought. Furthermore, when they came to encamp and lodge in the Medica, near to the Macedonians, who saw them so goodly great men, and so well trained and exercised in handling all kind[s] of weapons, so brave and lusty in words and threats against their enemies: they began to pluck up their hearts, and to look big, imagining that the Romans would never abide them, but would be afraid to look them in the face; and only to see their march, it was so terrible and fearful.

But Perseus, after he had encouraged his men in this sort, and had put them in such a hope and jollity, when **this barbarous supply** came to ask him a thousand crowns in hand for every captain, he was so **damped** and troubled withal in his mind, casting up the sum it came to, that [out of mere stinginess he drew back and let himself lose their assistance, as if he had been some **steward** [and] not the enemy of the Romans; and would have to give an exact account of the expenses of the war to those with whom he waged it.]

[omission for length]

But Perseus contrarily would not spend any part of his goods to save himself, his children and realm, but rather yielded to be led prisoner in triumph with a great ransom, to shew the Romans [what great riches he had **husbanded and preserved** for them.]

For he did not only send away the Gauls [that is, the Bastarnae] without giving them pay as he had promised; but, moreover, having persuaded **Gentius [the] king of Illyria** to take his part in these wars, for the sum of three hundred talents which he had promised to furnish him with: [he caused the money to be counted out in the presence of his messengers, and to be sealed up]. Whereupon Gentius thinking himself sure of the money promised, committed [a wicked and shameful act]: he seized and imprisoned the ambassadors sent to him from the Romans. Whence Perseus conclud[ed] that there was no need of money to make Gentius an enemy to the Romans, but that he [Gentius] had given] a **manifest** sign of his ill will towards them, and that it was to late to look back and repent him, now that his [flagrant injustice had sufficiently involved himself in the war]. So did he abuse the unfortunate king; and defrauded him of the three hundred talents he had promised him. And worse than this, shortly after[wards] he suffered Lucius Anicius, the Roman praetor, whom they sent against him with an army, to pluck King Gentius, his wife, and children, out of his realm and kingdom, and to carry them prisoners with him.

Narration and Discussion

Why was Aemilius so adamant that he must be fully in charge of the operation? How did the people react to this?

How did the stinginess or miserliness of Perseus end up being the one piece of good luck (vs. skill) that worked in Aemilius' favour?

For older students: Consider this idea: "So entirely did the people of Rome, that they might rule, and become masters of the world, yield obedience and service to reason and superior virtue." Do you agree with Plutarch's suggestion that willing submission to strong leaders was the key to Rome's long-term success?

Creative narration: Students might enjoy acting out the scene between Perseus and the mercenary soldiers, as he happily accepted their skill and muscle, but then backed off at the expense.

Lesson Five

Introduction

Lesson Five is the first of several lessons on the **Battle of Pydna**, which signified the takeover of Macedon by Rome.

Perseus and his troops had been encamped for some time in a strong position. Prior to Aemilius' arrival, he had beaten off other Roman attacks (see the end of **Lesson Three**), with troops that were strong and well-disciplined. However, things were about to change.

With such a long description of the battle, it is easy to become distracted by details of geography and military strategy. However, for the purposes of this study, try to focus on questions of character and leadership. How did Perseus and Aemilius each approach their tasks? How did they treat their own soldiers and their allies?

Vocabulary

in a place unpossible to be approached: that is, on the River Elpeus

dally: be in no hurry, waste time

by delay and expense: Perseus thought that Aemilius would eventually run short on supplies and/or money to pay the soldiers

it was not kept: it was unguarded

environ, encompass: surround

privy to his enterprise: informed of his plan

to get the top of the hill before them: to block their approach

repulsed their enemies: sent them back towards their camp

People

Nasica: A Roman politician (206-141 B.C.) who had married into the Scipio Africanus family. His full name was Publius Cornelius Scipio Nasica Corculum. Occasionally referred to as Scipio or Corculum, but usually called **Nasica,** meaning "pointy nose."

Scipio, Fabius Maximus: see introductory notes

Historic Occasions

168 B.C.: Battle of Pydna

On the Map

Perrhaebia was the northernmost region of **Thessaly**.

Reading

Part One

[Aemilius, coming against such an adversary, made light indeed of him, but admired his preparation and power.] For in one camp [Perseus] had four thousand horsemen, and no less than forty thousand footmen, with the which army he had planted himself alongst the seaside, by the foot of Mount Olympus, **in a place unpossible to be approached**: and there he had so well fortified all the straits and passages unto him with fortifications of wood, that he thought himself to lie safe out of all danger, and imagined [himself] to **dally** with Aemilius, [thinking **by delay and expense** to weary him out]. But [Aemilius], in the meantime, busy in thought, weighed all counsels and all means of attack; and perceiving his soldiers, from their former want of discipline, to be impatient of delay and ready on all occasions to teach their general his duty, [he] rebuked them, and bade them not meddle with what was not their concern], but to see their armour and weapon ready to serve valiantly, and to use their swords after the Roman fashion when their general should appoint and command them. Wherefore, to make them more careful to look to themselves, he commanded those that watched should have no spears nor pikes, because they should be more wakeful, having no long weapon to resist the enemy if they were assaulted.

[*omission for length*]

[Aemilius lay still for some days]; and it is said there were never seen two so great armies one so near to the other, and to be so quiet. [When he had tried and considered all things], he was informed of another way to enter into **Macedon**, through the country of **Perrhaebia** [*short omission*] where there lay no garrison; which gave him better hope to pass that way, for that **it was not kept**, than that he feared the narrowness and hardness of the way unto it.

So, [he proposed it for consultation. Amongst those that were present at the council, Scipio (surnamed **Nasica**, son-in-law to Scipio Africanus, who afterwards was so powerful in the senate-house) was the first that offered himself to command those that should be sent to encompass the enemy]. The second was **Fabius Maximus**, the eldest son of Aemilius, who being but a very young man, rose notwithstanding, and offered himself very willingly.

Aemilius was very glad of their offers; and gave them not so many men as Polybius writeth, but so many as Nasica himself declareth, in a letter of his he wrote to a king, where he reporteth all the story of this [expedition]. There were 3000 Italians levied in Italy, by the confederates of the Romans, who were not of the Roman legions; and in the left wing about 5000. Besides those, Nasica took also 120 men at arms, and about 200 Cretans and Thracians mingled together [*short omission*]. With this number Nasica departed from the camp, and took his way toward the seaside, and lodged by the Temple of Hercules, as if he had determined to do this feat by sea, to **environ** the camp of the enemies behind. But when the soldiers had supped, and that it was dark night, he made the captains of every band **privy to his enterprise**, and so marched all night [southwards], a contrary way from the sea, until at the length they came [to Pythion], where he lodged to rest the soldiers that were sore travelled.

[*omission: verses about the height of Mount Olympus*]

A Cretan deserted, who fled to the enemy during the march, [*and revealed*] to Perseus the design which the Romans had to **encompass** him; for he [Perseus], seeing that Aemilius lay still, had not suspected any such attempt.] He wondered much at these news; howbeit [he] removed not his camp from the place he lay in, but dispatched one of his captains called Milon, with ten thousand strangers, and two thousand Macedonians; and commanded him, with all the possible speed he could, **to get the top of the hill before them**.

Polybius sayeth that the Romans came and [attacked them] when they were sleeping. But Nasica writeth, that there was a marvellous sharp and terrible battle on the top of the mountain. [He] said plainly that a Thracian soldier coming towards him [Nasica], he threw his dart at him, and hitting him right in the breast, slew him stark dead; and, having **repulsed their enemies**, [and] Milon their captain shamefully running away in his coat without armour or weapon, he followed him without any danger; and so went down to the valley with the safety of all his company.

Narration and Discussion

What does it mean that the Roman soldiers were too ready "to teach their general his duty?" How did Aemilius rebuke them?

Explain the Roman strategy for surrounding the Macedonian army. Did it work?

Creative narration: Draw one of the scenes from this early part of the Battle of Pydna.

Lesson Six

Introduction

The skirmish at the top of the hill was only the beginning of the full Battle of Pydna. This lesson describes the preparation that went on after both sides had encamped near the plain chosen for battle.

Vocabulary

phalanx: the classic Macedonian battle formation using shields and spears.

joined with Nasica: Nasica's troops rejoined the main army

shewing a countenance: appearing

lodge, fortify the camp: set up camp and start building defenses

the hindmost: those at the rear

insensibly: little by little, without being noticed

the element: the sky, the heavens

novice: beginner, newcomer

hecatomb: the sacrifice of a hundred oxen

solemn sports: athletic games performed as a religious ritual

policy: strategy

procuring the skirmish: provoking a fight

foragers: those bringing in food and other supplies

greaves: leg armour

halberds: weapons resembling battleaxes

Reading

Part One

[*omission for length: Perseus, a little worried by the Roman attack, nevertheless moved his army to a plain south of Pydna, and prepared for battle there*]

[The place was a field fit for the action of a **phalanx**, which requires smooth standing and even ground; and [it] also had divers little hills, one joining another, [and] fit for the motions, whether in retreat or advance, of light troops and skirmishers.] There were two small rivers also, Aeson and Leucus, that ran through the same, the which, though they were not very deep, [it] being about the later end of the summer, yet they would annoy the Romans notwithstanding.

Now when Aemilius was **joined with Nasica**, he marched on straight in battle [ar]ray towards his enemies. But perceiving afar off their battle marched in very good order, and the great multitude of men placed in the same: he wondered to behold it; and suddenly stayed his army, considering with himself what he had to do. Then the young captains having charge under him, [eager to fight], went unto him to pray him to give the onset: but Nasica specially above the rest, having good hope in the former good luck he had at his first encounter.

Aemilius, smiling, answered him:

"So would I do, if I were as young as thou. But the
sundry victories I have won heretofore [have]
taught me by experience the faults the vanquished
do commit, [and forbid me to engage soldiers weary
with a long march against an army drawn up and
prepared for battle]."

When he had answered him thus, he commanded the first bands, that were now in view of the enemies, should embattle themselves, **shewing a countenance** to the enemy as though they would fight; and that those in the rearward should **lodge** in the meantime, and **fortify the camp**. [So that **the hindmost** in succession wheeling off by degrees and withdrawing, their whole order was **insensibly** broken up, and the army encamped without noise or trouble.]

Part Two

But when night came, and every man had supped, as they were going to sleep and take their rest: the moon which was at the full, and of a great height, began to darken, and to change into many sorts of colours, the moon losing her light, until such time as she vanished away, and was eclipsed altogether. Then the Romans began to make a noise with basins and pans, as their fashion is to do in such a chance, thinking by this sound to call her again, and to make her come to her light, lifting up many torches lighted, and firebrands into the air. The Macedonians on the other side did no such matter within their camp, but [they] were all together stricken with a horrible fear; and there ran straight a whispering rumour through the people, that this sign in **the element** signified the eclipse of the king.

[Aemilius was no **novice** in these things, nor was [he] ignorant of the nature of the seeming irregularities of eclipses—that in a certain revolution of time, the moon in her course enters the shadow of the earth and is there obscured, till, passing the region of darkness, she is again enlightened by the sun. Yet being a devout man, a religious observer of sacrifices and the art of divination, as soon as he perceived the moon beginning to regain her former luster, he offered up to her eleven heifers.] And the next morning also by the break of day, making sacrifice to Hercules, he could never have any signs or tokens that promised him good luck, in sacrificing twenty oxen one after another:

but at the one and twentieth, he had signs that promised him victory. [He then vowed a **hecatomb** and **solemn sports** to Hercules], and commanded his captains to put their men in readiness to fight.

Part Three

So [Aemilius] sought to win time, tarrying till the sun came about in the afternoon towards the west, to the end that the Romans, which were turned towards the east, should not have it in their faces when they were fighting. In the meantime, he reposed himself in his tent, which was all open behind towards the side that looked into the valley, where the camp of his enemies lay. When it grew towards night, to make the enemies set upon his men, some say he used this **policy**: he made a horse be driven towards them without a bridle, and certain Romans followed him, as [if] they would have taken him again: and this was the cause of **procuring the skirmish**. Other[s] say, that [some Thracians in Perseus' army] did set upon certain **foragers** of the Romans, that brought forage into the camp: out of the which, seven hundred of the Ligurians ran suddenly to the rescue, and relief coming still from both armies, at the last the main battle followed after.

Wherefore Aemilius, like a wise general, foreseeing by the danger of this skirmish, and the stirring of both camps, what the fury of the battle would come to: [he] came out of his tent, and passing by the bands, did encourage them, and prayed them to stick to it like men.

In the meantime, Nasica thrusting himself into the place where the skirmish was hottest, perceived the army of the enemies marching in battle, ready to join. The first [of the Macedonian army] that marched in the voward were the Thracians, who seemed terrible to look upon, as he writeth himself: for they were mighty made men, and carried marvellous bright targets of steel before them; their legs were armed with **greaves**, their coats were black, and [they] marched shaking heavy **halberds** upon their shoulders.

Next unto these Thracians, there followed them all the other strangers and soldiers whom the king had hired, diversely armed and set forth: for they were people of sundry nations gathered together, among whom the Paeonians were mingled.

The third squadron was of Macedonians, and all of them chosen men, as well for the flower of their youth, as for the valiantness of their persons: and they were all in goodly gilt armours, and [had] brave purple cassocks upon them, spick and span new. [As these were taking their places, they were followed from the camp by the troops in **phalanx** called the Brazen Shields, so that the whole plain seemed alive with the flashing of steel and the glistening of brass; and the hills also with their shouts, as they cheered each other on. In this order they marched, and with such boldness and speed, that those that were first slain died at but two furlongs' distance from the Roman camp.]

Narration and Discussion

In what ways did Aemilius show himself a wise general, even before the fighting began?

Compare the Roman and Macedonian reactions to the eclipse of the moon. Explain why Aemilius was "no novice in these things."

Creative narration: Draw your impressions of the approach of the Macedonian troops.

Lesson Seven

Introduction

The battle continued, and the Romans had a real challenge: breaking through the porcupine of spears and shields called a phalanx. At first it seemed that it couldn't be done; but then events began to turn.

Vocabulary

dissemble: conceal one's true feelings

bideth not: does not take one's part in

could make no breach into them: could not break past their defenses

ensign: flag or standard

press: crowd

rent: tore

corselet: piece of body armour

Reading

Part One

The charge being given, and the battle begun, Aemilius, galloping to the voward of his battle, perceived that the captains of the Macedonians which were in the first ranks had already thrust their pikes into the Romans' targets, so as they could not come near them with their swords; and that the other Macedonians, carrying their targets behind them, had now plucked them before them, and did base their pikes all at one time, and made a violent thrust into the targets of the Romans. [When Aemilius considered the great strength of this wall of shields, and the formidable appearance of a front thus bristling with arms, he was seized with amazement and alarm; nothing he had ever seen before had been equal to it; and in aftertimes he frequently used to speak both of the sight and of his own sensations. These, however, he **dissembled**, and rode through his army without either breastplate or helmet, with a serene and cheerful countenance.]

But on the contrary side, Perseus the king of Macedon, as Polybius writeth, so soon as the battle was begun, withdrew himself, and got into the city of Pydna, under pretense to go to do sacrifice unto Hercules: who doth not accept the faint sacrifice of cowards, neither doth receive their prayers, because they be unreasonable. For it is no reason that he that shooteth not should hit the white; nor that he should win the victory that **bideth not** the battle; neither that he should have any good that doeth nothing toward it; nor that a naughty man should be fortunate and prosper. The gods did favour Aemilius' prayers, because he prayed for victory with his sword in his hand, and, fighting, did call to them for aid.

Howbeit there is one Posidonius, a writer, who sayeth he [himself] was in that time, and, moreover, that he was at the battle; and he hath written a history containing many books of the acts of King Perseus, where he sayeth that it was not for faint heart, nor under colour to sacrifice unto Hercules, that Perseus went from the battle; but because he had a [kick from] a horse on the thigh the day before. Who though he could not very well help himself, and that all his friends sought to persuade him not to go to the battle: yet he caused one of his horse[s] to be brought to him notwithstanding (which he commonly used to ride up and down on), and taking his back, rode into the battle unarmed, [that amongst an infinite number of darts that flew about on all sides, one of iron lighted on him, and though not with the point, yet by a glance struck him with such force on his left side that it tore his clothes and so bruised his flesh that the mark remained a long time after. This is what Posidonius says in defense of Perseus].

Part Two

The Romans having their hands full, and being [so] stayed by the battle [array] of the Macedonians that they **could make no breach into them**: there was a captain of the Pelignians called Salius, who took the **ensign** of his [company], and cast it among the **press** of his enemies. Then all the Pelignians broke in upon them, with a marvellous force and fury into that place: for all Italians think it too great a shame and dishonour for soldiers to lose or forsake their ensign. Thus was there [a] marvellous force of both sides used in that place: for the Pelignians proved to cut the Macedonians' pikes with their swords, or else to make them give back with their great targets, or to make a breach into them, and to take the pikes with their hands.

But the Macedonians to the contrary, holding their pikes fast with both hands, ran them through that came near unto them: so that neither target nor corselet could hold out the force and violence of the push of their pikes, insomuch as they turned up the heels of the Pelignians and Marrucinians, who, like desperate beasts without reason, shutting in themselves among their enemies, ran willfully upon their own deaths, and their first rank were slain every man of them.

Thereupon, those that were behind gave back a little, but fled, not turning their backs; and only [retreated] towards Mount Olocrus. Aemilius, seeing that (as Posidonius writeth), **rent** his arming coat from his back for anger, because that some of his men gave back. Other[s] durst not front the battle of the Macedonians, which was so strongly embattled of every side, and so mured in with a wall of pikes, presenting their armed heads on every side a man could come, that it was impossible to break into them, no not so much as to come near them only.

Part Three

Yet notwithstanding, because the field was not altogether plain and even, the [Macedonian battle array] that was large in the front could not always keep that wall, continuing their targets close one to another; but they were driven of necessity to break and open in many places, as it happeneth oft in great battles, according to the great force of the soldiers: that in one place they thrust forward, and in another they give back, and leave a hole. Wherefore Aemilius suddenly taking the [ad]vantage of this occasion, [he] divided his men into small companies, and commanded them they should quickly thrust in between their enemies, and occupy the places they saw void in the front of their enemies, and that they should set on them in that sort, and not with one whole continual charge, but occupying them here and there with divers companies, in sundry places. Aemilius gave this charge unto the private captains of every band and their lieutenants; and the captains also gave the like charge unto their soldiers that could skillfully execute their commandment.

For they went presently into those parts where they saw the places open, and being once entered in among them, some gave charge upon the flanks of the Macedonians: [some on their sides where they were naked and exposed]; other[s] set upon them behind: so that the strength [of the phalanx] (which consisteth in keeping close together) being opened in this sort, was straight overthrown. Furthermore, when they came to fight man for man, or a few against a few: the Macedonians with their little short swords, came to strike upon the great shields of the Romans, which were very strong, and covered all their bodies down to the foot. And they, to the contrary, were driven of necessity to receive the blows of the strong heavy swords of the Romans upon their little weak targets: so that what with their heaviness, and the vehement force wherewith the blows lighted upon them, there was no target nor **corselet** but they passed it through, and ran them in. By reason whereof [the Macedonians] could make no long resistance, whereupon they turned their backs, and ran away.

[omission for length: the bravery of Marcus the son of Cato]

Then, singing a song of victory, the Romans went again more fiercely than before to give a charge upon their enemies, who were not yet broken asunder; until such time as, at the length, the three thousand chosen Macedonians fighting valiantly even to the last man, and never forsaking their ranks, were all slain in the place. After whose overthrow, there was a great slaughter of other[s] also that fled: so that all the valley and foot of the mountains thereabouts was covered with dead bodies.

Narration and Discussion

The force of the Macedonian phalanx "consists in common action and close union." How did the Romans break through?

An interesting statement: "The gods did favour Aemilius' prayers, because he prayed for victory with his sword in his hand . . ." Is there something here that could apply to Christian faith?

For older students: Should the Romans' victory be credited to their flexibility in fighting (such as their ability to move independently and to take advantage of gaps that opened between the phalanx and those fighting on either side); or was it due to poor Macedonian command?

Historical art: You may wish to look at the painting "Perseus Surrenders to Paulus," also called "King Perseus of Macedon in front of Aemilius Paulus," by Jean-François Pierre Peyron.

Lesson Eight

Introduction

The battle ended, but Aemilius feared that he had lost his favourite son, Scipio, in the battle. Scipio did show up eventually, which allowed the Romans to enjoy their victory over Macedon.

Vocabulary

new crept out of the shell: fresh-hatched, inexperienced

diminution: lessening

with his horsemen: Perseus' cavalry does not seem to have fought in the battle

diadem: crown

to be spoiled: as their reward

avarice and misery: greed and stinginess

sanctuary and privilege: those who flee to a sacred place are considered untouchable

lists or showplace: stadium

People

Scipio Africanus: see introductory note

Historic Occasions

147 B.C.: Destruction of Carthage by **Scipio Africanus**

134 B.C.: Defeat of Numantia under the command of **Scipio Africanus**

Reading

Part One

The next day after the battle, when the Romans did pass over the river of Leucus, they found it running all a-blood. For it is said there were slain at this field, of Perseus' men, above five and twenty thousand; and of the Romans' side, as Posidonius sayeth, not above six score; or as Nasica writeth, but fourscore only. And for so great an overthrow, it is reported it was wonderfully quickly done, and executed. For they began to fight about three of the clock in the afternoon, and had won the victory before four, and all the rest of the day they followed their enemies in chase, a hundred and twenty furlongs from the place where the battle was fought: so that it was very late, and far forth night, before they returned again into the camp.

So such as returned, were received with marvellous great joy [by] their pages that went out with links and torches lighted, to bring their masters into their tents, where their men had made great bonfires, and decked them up with crowns and garlands of laurel, saving the general's tent only: who was very heavy, for that of his two sons he brought with him to the wars, the younger could not be found, which he loved best of the [two], because he saw he was of a better nature than the rest of his brethren. For even then, being **new crept out of the shell** as it were, he was marvellous valiant and brave, and desired honour wonderfully.

Now Aemilius thought he had been cast away, fearing lest for lack of experience in the wars, and through the rashness of his youth, he had put himself too far in fight amongst the press of the enemies. Hereupon the camp heard straight what sorrow Aemilius was in, and how grievously he took it. The Romans, being set at supper, rose from their meat, and with torchlight some ran to Aemilius' tent, other[s] went out of the camp to seek [his son] among the dead bodies, if they might know him: so all the camp was full of sorrow and mourning, the valleys and hills all about did ring again with the cries of those that called "Scipio" aloud. For even from his childhood he had a natural gift in him, of all the rare and singular parts required in a captain and wise governor of the commonwealth above all the young men of his time.

At the last, when they were out of all hope of his coming again, he happily returned from the chase of the enemies, with two or three of his familiars only, all bloodied with new blood (like a swift running greyhound fleshed with the blood of the hare), having pursued very far for joy of the victory. It is that Scipio which afterwards destroyed both the cities of **Carthage** and **Numantium**; who was the greatest man of war, and [the] valiantest captain of the Romans in his time, and of the greatest authority and reputation among them. [Thus Fortune, deferring her displeasure and jealousy of such great success to some other time, let Aemilius at present enjoy this victory, without any detraction or **diminution**.]

Part Two

And as for Perseus, he fled first from the city of Pydna unto the city of Pella, **with his horsemen**, which were in manner all saved. Whereupon the [Macedonian] footmen that saved themselves by fleeing, meeting [the cavalry] by the way, called them traitors, cowards, and villains: and worse than that, they turned them off their horsebacks, and fought it out lustily with them. Perseus, [fearing the tumult], turned his horse out of the highway, and pulled off his purple coat, and carried it before him, and took [off] his **diadem**, fearing lest they should know him by these tokens; and because he might more easily speak with his friends by the way, he lighted a-foot, and led his horse [by] his hand.

But such as were about him, one made as though he would mend the latchet of his shoe, and other seemed to water his horse, another as though he would drink: so that one dragging after another in this sort, they all left him at the last, and ran their way, not fearing the enemies' fury so much as their king's cruelty: who, being grieved with his misfortune, sought to lay the fault of the overthrow upon all other[s] but himself. [Perseus arrived at Pella in the night, where Euctus and Eudaeus, two of his treasurers], came unto him, and speaking boldly (but out of time) presumed to tell him the great fault he had committed, and did counsel him also what he should do. The king was so moved with their presumption that with his own hands he stabbed his dagger in them both and slew them outright.

[*short omission for length*]

But when he was come into the city of Amphipolis, and afterwards into the city of Galepsus, and that the fear was well blown over: he returned again to his old humour, which was born and bred with him, and that was **avarice and misery**. For he made his complaint unto those that were about him, that he had un[a]wares given to the soldiers of Crete his plate and vessels of gold **to be spoiled**, being those which in old time belonged unto Alexander the Great: and [he] prayed them (with tears in his eyes) that had the plate, they would be contented to change it for ready money. Now such as knew his nature found straight this was but a [lie]; but those that trusted him, and did restore again the plate they had, did lose it every jot, for he never paid them [a] penny of it. So he got of his friends the value of thirty talents (which his enemies soon after did take from him). And with that sum he went into the isle of Samothracia, where he took the **sanctuary and privilege** of the temple of Castor and Pollux.

Part Three

They say that the Macedonians, of long continuance, did naturally love their kings; but then seeing all their hope and expectation broken, their hearts failed them, and broke withal. For they all came, and submitted themselves unto Aemilius, and made him lord of the whole realm of Macedon in two days; and this doth seem to confirm their words who impute all Aemilius' doings unto his good fortune.

And surely, the marvellous fortune he happened on in the city of Amphipolis, doth confirm it much, which a man cannot ascribe otherwise but to the special grace of the gods. For one day, beginning to do sacrifice, lightning fell from heaven, and set all the wood afire upon the altar, and sanctified the sacrifice. But yet the miracle of his fame is more to be wondered at. For four days after Perseus had lost the battle, and that the city of Pella was taken, as the people of Rome were at the **lists or showplace**, seeing horses run for games: suddenly there rose a rumour at the entering into the lists where the games were, how Aemilius had won a great battle of King Perseus, and had conquered all Macedon.

This news was rife straight in every man's mouth, and there followed upon it a marvellous joy and great cheer in every corner, with shouts and clapping of hands that continued all the day through the city of Rome. Afterwards they made diligent inquiry, how this rumour first came up; but no certain author could be known, and every man said they heard it spoken; so as in the end it came to nothing and passed away in that sort for a time.

[*omission for length*]

Narration and Discussion

Discuss this sentence: "Thus Fortune, deferring her displeasure and jealousy of such great success to some other time, let Aemilius at present enjoy this victory, without any detraction or diminution." Does this hint at trouble ahead for Aemilius?

Discuss how Perseus blamed others for his defeat. What did this show about his character?

Creative narration: Act out or write the part of a Roman scribe trying to track down the source of the news of the victory at Pydna.

Lesson Nine

Introduction

Instead of being pleased at having King Perseus throwing himself at his feet, Aemilius was angered and embarrassed, and had him taken away. Aemilius then headed to Greece, where he generously hosted games and banquets for the Macedonians . . . out of Perseus' treasury.

Vocabulary

vice: weakness, failure of character

sordid: dishonourable

exonerate: make free from guilt

your deserts: what you deserved

deprecate: despise, make less of

redoubted: dreaded, powerful

defrayed the whole charge thereof: paid for it

coffers of store: public treasury

concord: peace, harmony

People

Gnaeus Octavius: or Cnaeus Octavius; he became consul in 165 B.C.

Aelius Tubero: see introductory note

Nasica: see previous lessons

On the Map

Samothrace: an island in the North Aegean Sea

Reading

Part One

[**Gnaeus Octavius**, who was joined in command with Aemilius, came to an anchor with his fleet] under the isle of **Samothrace**, where he would not take Perseus by force out of the sanctuary where he was, for the reverence he did bear unto the gods Castor and Pollux; but he did besiege him in such sort, as he could not [e]scape him, nor flee by sea out of the island. [Notwithstanding, Perseus secretly persuaded Oroandes of Crete, master of a small vessel, to convey him and his treasure away. [Oroandes] [*brief omission*] took in the treasure, and] sent him word that he should not fail the next night following to come unto the pier by the temple of Ceres, with his wife, his children and servants; but the next night following [Oroandes] hoisted sail, and got him[self] away.

It was a pitiful thing that Perseus was driven to do and suffer at that time. For he came down in the night by ropes, out of a little strait window upon the walls; and not only himself, but his wife and little babes, who never knew before what fleeing and hardness meant. And yet he fetched a more grievous bitter sigh, when [some]one told him, on the pier, that he saw Oroandes the Cretan under sail in the main seas. Then day beginning to break, and seeing himself void of all hope, he ran with his wife for life to the wall, to recover the sanctuary again before the Romans that saw him could overtake him.

And as for his children, he had given them himself into the hands of one Ion [*brief omission*], who then did traitorously betray him: for [Ion] delivered [Perseus'] children unto the Romans. Which part was one of the chiefest causes that drove him (as a beast that will follow her little ones being taken from her) to yield himself into their hands that had his children. [His greatest confidence was in **Nasica**, and it was for him he called; but he not being there, he bewailed his misfortune, and, seeing there was no possible remedy, surrendered himself to **Octavius**.

And here, in particular, he made it manifest that he was possessed with a **vice** more **sordid** than covetousness itself: namely, the fondness of life; by which he deprived himself even of pity, the only thing that Fortune never takes away from the most wretched.]

For he made request they would bring him unto the general Aemilius; who rose from his chair when he saw him come, and went to meet him with his friends, the water standing in his eyes, to meet a great king, by fortune of war, and by the will of the gods, fallen into that most lamentable fact.

But [Perseus], to the contrary, unmanly and shamefully behaved himself. For he fell down at his feet, and embraced his knees, and uttered such uncomely speech and vile requests as Aemilius [him]self could not abide to hear them: but knitting his brows against him, being heartily offended, he spoke thus unto him:

> ["Why, unhappy man, do you thus take pains to
> **exonerate** Fortune of your heaviest charge against
> her, by conduct that will make it seem that you are
> not unjustly in calamity, and that it is not your
> present condition, but your former happiness, that
> was more than **your deserts**? And why
> **deprecate** also my victory, and make my
> conquests insignificant, by proving yourself a
> coward, and a foe beneath a Roman? Distressed
> valour challenges great respect, even from enemies;
> but cowardice, though never so successful, from the
> Romans has always met with scorn."]

Notwithstanding, he took him up, and taking him by the hand, gave him into the custody of **Tubero.**

Part Two

Then Aemilius went into his tent, and carried his sons, and sons-in-law with him, and other men of quality, and [e]specially the younger sort. And being sat down, he continued a great space very pensive with himself, not speaking a word: in so much as all the standers-by wondered much at the matter. In the end, he began to enter into discourse and talk of Fortune, and the unconstancy of these worldly things; and said unto them:

> "[Is it meet," said he, "for him that knows he is but man, in his greatest prosperity to pride himself and be exalted at the conquest of a city, nation, or kingdom, and not rather well to weigh this change of Fortune, in which all warriors may see an example of their common frailty, and learn a lesson that there is nothing durable or constant? For what time can men select to think themselves secure, when that of victory itself forces us more than any to dread our own fortune? And a very little consideration on the law of things, and how all are hurried round, and each man's station changed, will introduce sadness in the midst of greatest joy.] You see that in an hour's space we have trodden under our feet the house of Alexander the Great, who hath been the mightiest and most **redoubted** prince of the world. You see a king that not long since was followed and accompanied with many thousand soldiers of horsemen and footmen, brought at this present into such miserable extremity that he is enforced to receive his meat and drink daily at the hands of his enemies. Should we have any better hope, then, that Fortune will always favour our doings more than she doth his now, at this present? [No, young men, cast off that vain pride and empty boast of victory; sit down with humility, looking always for what is yet to come, and the possible future reverses which the divine displeasure may eventually make the end of our present happiness.]"

Such were Aemilius' words to these young men, as it is reported, bridling, by these and such like persuasions, the lusty bravery of this youth, even as with the bit and bridle of reason.

Part Three

[*omission for length: Aemilius' journey through Greece, during which he re-established city governments and gave gifts to the people*]

Afterwards when the ten ambassadors were arrived that were sent from Rome to establish with him the realm of Macedon, he redelivered the Macedonians their country and towns again, to live at liberty, according to their laws, paying yearly to the Romans, for tribute, a hundred talents: where before they were wont to pay unto their kings ten times as much. And he made plays and games of all sorts; and did celebrate sumptuous sacrifices unto the gods. He kept open court to all comers, and made noble feasts, and **defrayed the whole charge thereof** with the treasure Perseus had gathered together, sparing for no cost. But through his care and foresight there was such a special good order taken, every man so courteously received and welcomed, and so orderly marshalled at the table according to their estate and calling, that the Greeks wondered to see him so careful in matters of sport and pleasure; and that he took as great pains in his own person to see that small matters should be ordered as they ought, as he took great regard for discharge of more weighty causes. But this was a marvellous pleasure to him, to see that among such sumptuous sights prepared to shew pleasure to the persons invited, no sight or stately shew did so delight them as to enjoy the sight and company of his person. So he told them that seemed to wonder at his diligence and care in these matters that to order a feast well required as great judgement and discretion, as to set a battle: to make the one fearful to the enemies, and the other acceptable to his friends.

But men esteemed his bounty and magnanimity for his best virtue and quality. For he did not only refuse to see the king's wonderful treasure of gold and silver; but caused it to be delivered to the custody of the treasurers, to carry to the **coffers of store** in Rome; and only suffered his sons, that were learned, to take the books of the king's library. When he did reward the soldiers for their valiant service in this battle, he gave his son-in-law **Aelius Tubero** a cup weighing five talents. It is the same Tubero we told you of before, who lived with sixteen other[s] of his kin all in one house, and the only revenue they had [that of] a little farm in the country. Some say that cup was the first piece of plate that ever came into the house of the Aelians, and yet it came for honour and reward of virtue; but before that time, neither themselves, nor their wives, would ever have, or wear, any gold or silver.

After he had very well ordered and disposed all things, at the last he took leave of the Greeks, and counselled the Macedonians to remember the liberty the Romans had given them, and that they should be careful to keep it by their good government and **concord** together.

Narration and Discussion

Discuss Aemilius' response to Perseus' groveling, especially this saying: "Distressed valour challenges great respect, even from enemies; but cowardice, though never so successful, from the Romans has always met with scorn." **Creative narration:** This might be an interesting scene to act out or write in dramatic form.

What point did Aemilius make about gloating over a victory?

For older students: Did the Romans truly give the Macedonians liberty?

Lesson Ten

Introduction

When the army returned to Rome, the soldiers immediately began to grumble about the tiny reward they were given for their part in those attacks. This escalated into a vote as to whether Aemilius should be allowed his triumph at all; but a speech by **Marcus Servilius** decided the question.

Vocabulary

commission: orders

spoil: raid, ransack, loot

policy: strategy, trick

the honour of triumph: the right to have a public victory celebration

calumnies: lies

sought no redress: did nothing about it

betimes: quickly, in short order

stay to take the voices of the people: not accept the vote

People

Servius Galba: Servius Sulpicius Galba, who was later elected consul

Marcus Servilius: Marcus Servilius Pulex Geminus, a Roman statesman

Historic Occasions

167 B.C.: Roman attack on Epirus

On the Map

Epirus: a region of southeastern Europe, between the Pindus Mountains and the Ionian Sea

Reading

Part One

Then he departed from them, and took his journey towards the country of **Epirus**, having received **commission** from the senate of Rome to suffer his soldiers, who had done service in the battle and overthrow of King Perseus, to **spoil** all the cities of that country. Wherefore that he might surprise them on a sudden, and that they should mistrust nothing, he sent to all the cities that they should send him, by a certain day, ten of the chiefest men of every city. Who, when they were come, he commanded them to go and bring him, by such a day, all the gold and silver they had within their cities, as well in their private houses as in their temples; and [he] gave unto every one of them a captain and garrison with them, as if it had been only to have received and searched for the gold and silver he demanded.

But when the day appointed was come, the soldiers in divers places (and all at one time) set upon their enemies; and did rifle and spoil them of that [which] they had; and made them also pay ransom [for] every man. So as by this **policy**, there were taken and made slaves, in one day, a hundred and fifty thousand persons, and three score and ten cities spoiled and sacked every one. [Yet what was given to each soldier, out of so vast a destruction and utter ruin, amounted to no more than eleven drachmas; so that men could only] fear the terror of the wars, to see the wealth and riches of so great a realm to amount to so little for every man's share.

Part Two

When Aemilius had done this [deed] against his own nature (which was very gentle and courteous), he went unto the seaside to the city of Oricus, and there embarked with his army bound for Italy.

Where when he was arrived, he went up the Tiber River against the [current], in King Perseus' chief galley, which had sixteen oars on a side, richly set out with the armour of the prisoners, rich clothes of purple colour, and other such spoils of the enemies: so that the Romans [were] running out of Rome in multitudes to see this galley, and going side by side by her as they rowed softly, Aemilius took as great pleasure in it as in any open games, or feasts, or triumph that had been showed indeed.

But when the soldiers saw that the gold and silver of King Perseus' treasure was not divided amongst them, according unto promise; and that they had a great deal less than they looked for, they were marvellously offended, and inwardly grudged Aemilius in their hearts. Nevertheless they [dared] not speak it openly; but did accuse him that he had been too strait unto them in this war, and therefore they did shew no great desire, nor forwardness, to procure him **the honour of triumph**.

[When **Servius Galba**, who was Aemilius' enemy (though he commanded as tribune under him) understood this, he had the boldness plainly to affirm that a triumph was not to be allowed him; and [he] sowed various **calumnies** amongst the soldiers, which yet further increased their ill-will. Nay, more, he desired the tribunes of the people, because the four hours that were remaining of the day could not suffice for the accusation, to let him put it off till another.] The tribunes made him answer that he should speak then what he had to say against him [Aemilius], or otherwise they would not grant him audience. Hereupon [Galba] began to make a long oration in his dispraise, full of railing words; and spent all the rest of the day in that railing oration. Afterwards, when night came on, the tribunes broke up the assembly; and the next morning, the soldiers being encouraged by Galba's oration, and having confedered together, did flock about Galba, in the mount of the Capitol, where the tribunes had given warning [*that*] they would keep their assembly.

Part Three

Now [it] being broad day, Aemilius' triumph was referred to the most number of voices of the people; and the first tribe flatly did deny his triumph. The senate, and the residue of the people, hearing that, were very sorry to see they did Aemilius so open wrong and **injury**. The common people said nothing to it; but seemed to be very sorry; howbeit they **sought no redress**.

The lords of the senate cried out upon them, and said it was too much shame, and exhorted one another to bridle the insolency and boldness of these soldiers, who would grow in the end to such tumult and disorder that they would commit all mischief and wickedness, if **betimes** they were not looked to and prevented, seeing they did so openly stand against their general, seeking to deprive him of the honour of his triumph and victory. So they assembled a good company of them together, and went up to the Capitol, and prayed the tribunes they would **stay to take the voices of the people** until they had acquainted them with such needful matter as they had to open unto them. The tribunes granted to it, and silence was made.

Then **Marcus Servilius**, who had been consul, and had fought three and twenty combats of life and death in his own person, and had always slain as many of his enemies as challenged him man for man, rose up and spoke in favour of Aemilius in this manner:

"I know now," (said he) "better than before, how
noble and worthy a captain Aemilius Paulus is; who
hath achieved such glory and honourable victory,
with so dishonourable and disobedient soldiers.
And I can but wonder that the people, [who] not
long since rejoiced and made great account of the
victories and triumphs won upon the Illyrians and
other nations of Africa; and that now they should
for spite envy his glory (doing what lieth in them to
hinder) to bring a Macedonian king alive in a
triumph; and to shew the glory and greatness of
King Philip and Alexander the Great subdued by the
Romans' force and power. What reason have ye,
that not long since, upon a flying rumour that
Aemilius had won the battle against Perseus, you
straight made sacrifices to the gods with great joy,
praying them that you might be witnesses of the
truth thereof; and now that the person himself
whom you made general is returned home, and
doth deliver you most assured victory, you do
frustrate the gods' most solemn thanks and honour
due to them, and do deprive yourselves also of your
wonted glory in such a case? as if you were afraid to
see the greatness of your prosperity, or that you
meant to pardon a king, your slave and prisoner.
[And of the two, much better were it to put a stop to
the triumph out of pity to [Perseus], than out of
envy to your general; yet to such a height of power
is malice arrived amongst you, that a man without
one scar to show on his skin, that is smooth and
sleek with ease and home-keeping habits, will
undertake to define the office and duties of a
general, before us who with our own wounds have
been taught how to judge of the valour or the

cowardice of commanders.]"

And speaking these words, he cast open his gown, and showed before them all the infinite scars and cuts he had received upon his breast: and then turning him behind, showed all such places as were not fit to be seen openly, and so [he] turned him again to Galba, and said unto him:

> "Thou mockest me for that I shew thee: but I rejoice
> before my country men and citizens: that for
> serving my country night and day a-horseback, I
> have these wounds upon me which thou seest. Now
> get thee about thy business, and receive their
> voices; and I will come after, noting them that are
> naughty and unthankful citizens, who like to be
> soothed with flattery, and not stoutly commanded,
> as behoveth a general in the war."

These words so reined the hard-headed soldiers with the curb of reason that all the other tribes agreed [as] one; and granted Aemilius [his] triumph.

Narration and Discussion

Does Plutarch feel that the sacking of the cities was worth it for a reward of only eleven drachmas apiece? What do you think? (Would he have approved of it more if the reward had been greater?)

Creative narration: What a great scene Part Two would be for acting out! There is of course the difficulty of needing great numbers of Romans! Could you find a way around it?

Lesson Eleven

Introduction

The Romans staged a three-day parade (a **triumph**) in honour of Aristides and the victory over Perseus.

Vocabulary

scaffolds: raised seating

sarissas: long spears

frocks: uniforms, costumes

basins for libation: vessels for drink offerings to the gods

to make one among…: to be one more piece of the "loot"

passing sumptuously: quite lavishly

merry pleasant toys: good-natured jesting, teasing

Historic Occasions

167 B.C.: Aemilius' return to Rome

Reading

Part One

The order and solemnity [of Aemilius' triumph] was performed in this sort. [The people erected **scaffolds** in the Forum, in the circuses (as they call their buildings for horse-races), and in all other parts of the city where they could best behold the show. The spectators were clad in white garments; all the temples were open, and full of garlands and perfumes; the ways were cleared and kept open by numerous officers, who drove back all who crowded into or ran across the main avenue.]

Furthermore, the sight of this triumph was to continue three days, whereof the first was scant sufficient to see the passing by of the images, tables, and pictures, and statues of wonderful bigness, all won and gotten of their enemies, and drawn upon two hundred and fifty chariots.

The second day, there were carried, upon a number of carts, all the fairest and richest armour of the Macedonians, [both of brass and steel], all glistering bright, being newly furbished and [arranged purposely with the greatest art, so as to seem to be tumbled in heaps carelessly and by chance]. [There were helmets thrown upon shields; coats of mail,] greaves, Cretan targets, Thracian bucklers, and quivers of arrows lay huddled amongst horses' bits; and through these there appeared the points of naked swords, intermixed with long Macedonian **sarissas**.] All this armour and carriage [was] bound one to another so trimly (neither being too loose, nor too strait) that one hitting against another, as they drew them upon the carts through the city, they made such a sound and noise, as it was fearful to hear it: [so that, even as spoils of a conquered enemy, they could not be beheld without dread].

After these carts laden with armour, there followed three thousand men, which carried the ready money in seven hundred and fifty vessels, which weighed about three talents apiece, and every one of them [was] carried by four men. [Others brought silver bowls and goblets and cups, all disposed in such order as to make the best show, and all curious as well for their size as the solidity of their embossed work.]

Part Two

The third day, early in the morning, the trumpets began to sound and set forwards, sounding no march nor sweet note, to beautify triumph withal: but they blew out the brave alarm they sound at an assault, to give the soldiers courage for to fight. [Next followed young men wearing **frocks** with ornamented borders, who led to the sacrifice a hundred and twenty stalled oxen, with their horns gilded, and their heads adorned with ribbons and garlands; and with these were boys that carried **basins for libation**, of silver and gold. After this was brought the gold coin, which was divided into vessels that weighed three talents, like those that contained the silver; they were in number seventy-seven. These were followed by those that brought the consecrated bowl which Aemilius had caused to be made, that weighed ten talents, and was set with precious stones.] And next unto them went other that carried plate, made and wrought after [the] antique fashion, and notable cups of the ancient kings of Macedon: [such] as the cup [of] Antigonus, and another [of] Seleucus; and, to be short, all the whole cupboard of plate of gold and silver of King Perseus.

And next them came the chariot of his armour, in the which was all King Perseus' harness, and his royal [diadem] upon his armour.

And a little space between them, followed next the king's children, whom they led prisoners, with the train of their schoolmasters and other officers, and their servants, weeping and lamenting: who held up their hands unto the people that looked upon them, and taught the king's young children to do the like, to ask mercy and grace at the people's hands. There were three pretty little children, two sons and a daughter amongst them, whose tender years and lack of understanding, made them (poor souls) they could not feel their present misery, which made the people so much more to pity them, when they saw the poor little infants, that they knew not the change of their hard fortune: so that for the compassion they had of them, they almost let the father pass without looking upon him. Many people's hearts did melt for very pity, that the tears ran down their cheeks, so as this sight brought both pleasure and sorrow together to the lookers-on, until they were past and gone a good way out of sight.

King Perseus, the father, followed after his children and their train; and he was clothed in a black gown, wearing a pair of slippers on his feet after his country manner. He showed by his countenance his troubled mind, oppressed with sorrow of his most miserable state and fortune. He was followed with his kinfolks, his familiar friends, his officers and household servants, their faces disfigured by blubbering, shewing to the world by their lamenting tears and sorrowful eyes cast upon their unfortunate master, how much they sorrowed and bewailed his most hard and cursed fortune, little accounting of their own misery.

The voice goeth that Perseus sent unto Aemilius, to entreat him that he should not be led through the city in the show and sight of the triumph. But Aemilius mocking (as he deserved) his cowardly faint heart, answered: "As for that, it was before, and is now in him, to do if he will." Meaning to let him understand thereby, that he might rather choose to die, than, living, to receive such open shame. Howbeit his heart would not serve him; he was so cowardly [*brief omission*] that he was contented **to make one among his own spoils**.

After all this, there followed four hundred princely crowns of gold, which the cities and towns of Greece had purposely sent by their ambassadors unto Aemilius, to honour his victory: and next unto them, he came himself in his chariot triumphing, which was **passing sumptuously** set forth and adorned. It was a noble sight to behold: and yet the person of himself only was worth the looking on, without all that great pomp and magnificence. For he was appareled in a purple gown [interwoven] with gold, and [he] carried in his right hand a laurel bough, as all his army did besides: the which being divided by bands and companies, followed the triumphing chariot of their captain, [with] some of the soldiers singing songs of victory, which the Romans use to sing in like triumphs, mingling them with **merry pleasant toys**, rejoicing at their captain. Other[s] of them also did sing songs of triumph, in the honour and praise of Aemilius' noble conquest and victory. He was openly praised, blessed, and honoured of everybody, and neither hated nor envied of honest men. [Except so far as it seems the province of some god to lessen that happiness which is too great and inordinate, and so to mingle the affairs of human life that no one should be entirely free and exempt from calamities; but, as we read in Homer, that those should think themselves truly blessed to whom Fortune has given an equal share of good and evil.].

Narration and Discussion

Did Perseus have a choice about being part of the spectacle? What do you think of the choice he made?

Creative narration: Describe the triumph in any way you want: verbally, in a drawing, with a song of celebration, or in some other way.

For older students: Some people believe that after a run of "good luck," any person (or economy, or sports team) may be due for a change in fortune. Does this differ from a Christian perspective?

Lesson Twelve and Examination Questions

Introduction

The hint that nothing could remain perfect was fulfilled, as two of Aemilius' sons died at the time of his triumph. But he accepted his loss philosophically. ("I knew something bad would probably happen, so

I'm just glad it happened to me personally and not to Rome.") The rest of the passage describes Aemilius' time as censor, his retirement years, and his final return to Rome.

Vocabulary

replenished: filled

favourable gale: helpful wind

unlucky or sinister: negative

countervailed: offset

censor: see introductory notes

bier: the framework for carrying a corpse

Historic Occasions

166 B.C.: death of Perseus

164 B.C.: Aemilius elected censor

160 B.C.: death of Aemilius Paulus

Reading

Part One

[Aemilius had four sons, of whom Scipio and Fabius, as is already related, were adopted into other families; the other two, whom he had by a second wife, and who were yet but young, he brought up in his own house. One of these died at fourteen years of age, five days before his father's triumph; the other at twelve, three days after; so that there was no Roman without a deep sense of his suffering, and who did not shudder at the cruelty of Fortune, that had not scrupled to bring so much sorrow into a house **replenished** with happiness, rejoicing, and sacrifices; and to intermingle tears and laments with songs of victory and triumph. Aemilius, however, reasoning justly that courage and resolution was not merely to resist armour and spears, but all the shocks of ill-fortune, so met and so adapted himself to these mingled and contrasting circumstances, so as to outbalance the evil with the good, and his private concerns with those of the public; and thus did not allow anything either to take away from the grandeur or sully the dignity of his victory.] For when he had buried the eldest of his two last sons, he [waited] not to make his triumphant entry, as you have heard before. And his second son also being deceased after his triumph, he caused the people to assemble, and in face of the whole made an oration, [not like a man that stood in need of comfort from others, but one that undertook to support his fellow-citizens in their grief for the sufferings he himself underwent.]

> "I," he said, "who never yet feared anything that was human, have, amongst such as were divine, always had a dread of Fortune as faithless and inconstant; and, for the very reason that in this war she had been as a **favourable gale** in all my affairs, I still expected some change and reflux of things. In one day I passed the Ionian sea, and reached Corcyra from Brundisium; thence in five more I sacrificed at Delphi, and in other five days came to my forces in Macedonia, where, after I had finished the usual sacrifices for the purifying of the army, I entered on my duties; and, in the space of fifteen days, put an honourable period to the war.] But yet, mistrusting Fortune always, being the prosperous course of my affairs, and considering that there were no other enemies, nor dangers I needed to fear: I feared sorely she would change at my return, when I should be upon the sea, bringing home so goodly and victorious an army, with so many spoils and so many princes and kings taken prisoners. And yet when I was safely arrived in the haven, and seeing all the city at my return full of joy, and of feasts and sacrifices: I still suspected Fortune, knowing her manner well enough, that she useth not to gratify men so frankly, nor to grant them so great things clearly, without some certain spark of envy waiting on them. [Nor could my mind, that was still as it

were, in labour, and always foreseeing something to befall this city, free itself from this fear, until this great misfortune befell me in my own family; and till, in the midst of those days set apart for triumph, I carried two of the best of sons, my only destined successors, one after another to their funerals.] Wherefore, methinks now I may say, I am out of all danger, at the least touching my chiefest and greatest misfortune: and do begin to [e]stablish myself with this assured hope, that this good Fortune henceforth shall remain with us evermore, without fear of other **unlucky or sinister** chance. For she hath sufficiently **countervailed** the favourable victory she gave you, with the envious mishap wherewith she hath plagued both me and mine: shewing the conqueror and triumpher as noble an example of man's misery and weakness, as the party conquered that had been led in triumph. Saving that Perseus yet, conquered as he is, hath this comfort left him: to see his children living, and that the conqueror, Aemilius, hath lost his."

[omission for length: the imprisonment and death of Perseus]

Part Two

But Aemilius also, although he took ever the noblemen's part, was not therefore less beloved of the common people than those that always flattered them, doing all things as the people would, to please them: which the common people did witness, as well by other honours and offices they offered him, as in the dignity of the **censor** which they gave him. For it was the holiest office of all other at that time, and of greatest power and authority, specially for inquiry and reformation of every man's life and manners.

[omission for length]

And after he had ordered and disposed the greatest matters of his charge and office, he fell sick of a disease that, at the beginning, seemed very dangerous; but in the end there was no other danger, saving that it was a lingering disease, and hard to cure. So, following the counsel of physicians, who willed him to go to a city in Italy called Velia, he took sea, and went thither, and continued there a long time, dwelling in pleasant houses upon the seaside, quietly and out of all noise. But during this time of his absence, the Romans wished for him many a time and oft. And when they were gathered together in the theaters, to see the plays and sports, they cried out divers times for him: whereby they showed that they had a great desire to see him again.

Time being come about when they used to make a solemn yearly sacrifice, and Aemilius finding himself also in good perfect health: he returned again to Rome, where he made the sacrifice with the other priests, all the people of Rome gathering about him, rejoicing much to see him. The next day after, he made another particular sacrifice, to give thanks unto the gods for recovery of his health. After the sacrifice was ended, he went home to his house, and sat him down to dinner: he suddenly fell into a raving (without any perseverance of sickness spied in him before, or any change or alteration in him) and his wits went from him in such sort that he died within three days after, lacking no necessary thing that an earthly man could have to make him happy in this world. [Nay, his very funeral pomp had something in it remarkable and to be admired, and his virtue was graced with the most solemn and happy rites at his burial; consisting, not in gold and ivory, or in the usual sumptuousness and splendor of such preparations, but in the good-will, honour, and love, not only of his fellow-citizens, but of his enemies themselves.]

For all those that met in Rome by chance at that time, that were either come out of Spain, from Liguria, or out of Macedon, all those that were young and strong [took up the **bier** and carried it]; and the old men followed his body to accompany the same, calling Aemilius the benefactor, saviour, and father of their country. For he did not only entreat them gently and graciously, whom he had subdued: but all his lifetime he was ever ready to [do them good], and to set forward their causes, even as [if] they had been his confederates, very friends, and near kinsmen. [They report that the whole of his estate scarce amounted to three hundred and seventy thousand drachmas; to which he left his two sons [as] co-heirs; but Scipio, who was the youngest, being adopted into the more wealthy family of Africanus, gave it all to his brother.

Such are said to have been the life and manners of Aemilius.]

Narration and Discussion

Discuss Aemilius' speeches about courage and resolution. How did his actions show that he believed in what he said? Is it true "that Fortune never conferred any great benefits that were unmixed and unattended with probabilities of reverse?" (Consider Romans 8:28.)

What do you think are the most significant points Plutarch brings out about the death and funeral of Aemilius? How do they reflect his life?

Examination Questions

Younger Students:

1. How did Aemilius conduct the war against the Ligurians at the time of an eclipse of the moon?

2. (Alternate) Describe (a), how Perseus was betrayed by Oroandes, yielded himself to the Romans, and was brought before Aemilius; or, (b), the triumph which the Romans gave.

Older Students:

1. a) Describe the speech of Aemilius on the death of his two sons.
    b) Describe the triumph of Aemilius after his victory over Perseus.

2. (For high school students) Contrast, in the manner of Plutarch, the characters of Aemilius and Perseus. Give incidents as illustration.

Aristides

(530-468 B.C.)

Who was Aristides?

Aristides (nicknamed Aristides the Just) was an Athenian statesman and general during the Persian Wars. He led the Athenians at the Battle of Marathon; fought at Salamis; and then led the Athenian forces at Plataea, the final battle against the Persians. Aristides was a creative and gifted leader, whose concern with justice led him to solve problems in unusual ways.

How do you pronounce Aristides?

Arr-i-STYE-deez.

Who were the rulers in Athens?

The council of elders in Athens was the **Areopagus.** It was made up of men who had held high public office, such as **archon**, much like the Roman Senate. Over the years, the council held less actual power, and more decisions were made by the **archons.**

The word **archon** simply means ruler, and it could be applied to anything from the leader of a small group to the governor of a state. The top ruler of Athens was the eponymous archon (**archon eponymos**), who was elected for a term of one year. The word is often translated "chief magistrate," but North translates it as **mayor** or **provost**. Aristides was **archon eponymos** for the year 489-488.

Who was Themistocles?

Themistocles was an Athenian general and statesman who lived from approximately 524-459 B.C. He is the subject of Plutarch's *Life of Themistocles*, and there is much more to his story than can be addressed here. One note of interest is that when he fled from Greece in the year 472 or 471 B.C., he was given sanctuary by Alexander I of Macedon, who appears here in **Lesson Seven**.

Who was Pausanias?

Pausanias was the military commander of the Spartans (Lacedaemonians). After the Persian Wars, he was accused of conspiring with King Xerxes to put Sparta under Persian control. He died in 470 B.C. after an accusation of treason.

Top Ten Terms in Aristides

If you recognize these words, you're well on your way to mastering North's vocabulary. (They will not be noted in the lessons.)

1. **Acquaint:** To **acquaint** is used several times in the story, meaning either "to become used to, familiar with" or "to share information."

2. **Divers:** several

3. **Engage:** fight with

4. **Footmen:** foot soldiers

5. **Spoil or spoils:** treasure seized from an enemy; loot

6. **Stay:** delay, detain, stop

7. **Strait:** tight, narrow. To be **strait** with people means to be restrictive or stingy. A **strait** is a narrow channel of water.

8. **Strange:** usually means "foreign," but sometimes just means "strange." Soldiers that are **strangers** are often foreign mercenaries (soldiers employed by any army that will pay them).

9. **Succour:** aid, help

10. **Target:** shield

    Bonus phrase: "The barbarous people" or **barbarians** usually refers to the **Persians**, who are sometimes called the **Medes**.

Lesson One

Plutarch begins this *Life* with a question: was Aristides rich or poor, and what evidence do we have on either side? For instance, someone says that Aristides must have been rich because he sponsored theatrical performances. Plutarch answers that it wasn't uncommon in those days for someone like Aristides both to receive gifts of money and to spend them on something for the public benefit.

As another example, Aristides was ostracized at one time; and, as Plutarch says, ostracism (oddly enough) was considered too good for common people; so some would think that Aristides must have belonged to a wealthy family. But Plutarch says that "everyone was liable to it whom his reputation, birth, or eloquence raised above the common level."

So was Aristides one of the privileged upper class, or someone who rose by his own merits (or by the hand of "Fortune")?

Vocabulary

mayor or provost: archon eponymos; see introductory note

drawing of the bean: drawing lots; **by lot of beans** is the equivalent of "by luck of the draw"

wonted: usual

rate: tax assessment

ostracism, "Ostracismon": a formal procedure of banishment

three-footed stools: pedestals. Dryden translates it "tripods."

they themselves had borne the charge: they had paid for the dramatic productions or games

voices: a vote

Historic Occasions

530 B.C.: birth of Aristides

525 B.C.: Persians seized Egypt

On the Map

You will find the city of Athens on any map of Greece; but the best one for our purposes will show it at around 500 B.C. or slightly later.

Reading

Aristides, the son of Lysimachus, was certainly of the tribe of Antiochides, and of the town of Alopecia. [As to wealth, statements differ]: some say he lived poorly all the days of his life, and that he left two daughters, which by reason of their poverty lived unmarried many years after their father's death. And many of the oldest writers do confirm that for truth.

Yet Demetrius Phalerius [*the Phalerian*], in his book entitled *Socrates*, writeth the contrary: that he knew certain lands Aristides had in the village of Phaleria, which did yet bear the name of "Aristides' lands," in the which his body is buried. And furthermore, to show that he was well to live, and that his house was rich and wealthy, he bringeth forth these proofs.

First, that he was one year **mayor or provost** of Athens (called "Archon Eponymos"), because the year took the name of him that had it yearly. And they say he came to it by **drawing of the bean**, according to the ancient use of the Athenians, and their **wonted** manner of making their election of the said office. In [this] election none were admitted to draw the bean but such as were [of the highest assessed families], according to the value and **rate** of their goods [*brief omission*].

Secondly, [Demetrius] allegeth [that Aristides] was banished by the **ostracism**, which banisheth the nobility and great rich men only, whom the common people envy because of their greatness; and never dealeth with poor men. The third and last reason he makes is that he left, [as a] gift, **three- footed stools** in the temple of Bacchus, which those do commonly offer up [who] have won the victory in comedies, tragedies, or other such like pastimes, whereof **they themselves had borne the charge**. And those three-footed stools remain there yet, which they say were given by Aristides, and have this inscription upon them: "The tribe of Antiochides won the victory, Aristides defrayed the charges of the games, and Archestratus the Poet taught them to play his comedies." This last reason, though it seem[s] likeliest of them all, yet is it the weakest of the rest. For Epaminondas, (whom every man knoweth was poor even from his birth, and always lived in great poverty), and Plato the Philosopher [both took on] the charges of games that were of no small expense, the one having borne the charges of flute players at Thebes, and the other the dance of the children which danced in a round at Athens: towards the furnishing of which charges Dion the Syracusan gave Plato money, and Pelopidas also gave Epaminondas money.

[*omission for length*]

But for the **"Ostracismon"** banishment, it is true that such as were great men in estimation above the common people, either in fame, nobility, or eloquence, they only were subject unto this banishment. For Damon himself, being Pericles' schoolmaster, was banished, only because the common people thought him too wise. Moreover, Idomeneus writeth that Aristides was their provost for a year, not by **lot of beans** but by **voices** of the Athenians that chose him. And if he were provost since the [Battle of Plataea], as Demetrius writeth, it is likely enough that they did him this honour for his great virtue and notable service, which other[s] were wont to obtain for their riches.

[*short omission*]

Narration and Discussion

Much of this section is a weighing of evidence for or against the fact of Aristides' supposed poverty. What are the arguments on each side, and how does Plutarch answer them?

For older students: Look up the roots of the word "virtuous." How did the ancient Greeks and Romans understand "virtue?" In their thinking (and in your own), could a rich man be virtuous? Could a poor man be virtuous? Is poverty itself a virtue?

Lesson Two

Introduction

This lesson introduces **Themistocles**, a leader in Athens with whom Aristides shared a lifelong friendship/enemyship. (See the introductory notes for this study.) The two had almost nothing in common, including temperament, political beliefs, and moral philosophy. Themistocles was an innovator and a take-charge leader, and he couldn't understand why it wouldn't be right to show favouritism to friends. He also stood for democracy in government. Aristides, on the other hand, set justice and integrity above popularity; but preferred **aristocratical** rule, or oligarchy.

Vocabulary

aristocratical: supporting the rule of the old, noble families

populace: common people

subtle: the opposite of straightforward; sly

staid: unwavering, steady; perhaps unadventurous

preferment: advancement in position

indifferent and not partial: not showing favouritism

tribunal: court of justice

stand upon his friends: depend on their influence (and therefore owe them favours in return)

bearing themselves upon their friends: similarly, using their connections to influence decisions or gain advancement

withstanding: standing against him

preferred: proposed

Themistocles' purpose took no place: the thing he proposed was not accepted

gaining the day: winning

commendation: praise

People

Cleisthenes: the founder of Athenian democracy

Lycurgus: lawgiver in Sparta (**Lacedaemonia**) in the eighth century B.C.; the subject of Plutarch's *Life of Lycurgus*

Historic Occasions

510 B.C.: Expulsion of the tyrants from Athens

509 B.C.: Reforms of Cleisthenes

Reading

Part One

[Aristides being the friend and supporter of that **Cleisthenes** who settled the government after the expulsion of the tyrants; and emulating and admiring **Lycurgus** the **Lacedaemonian** above all politicians; [he] adhered to the **aristocratical** principles of government; and had Themistocles, son to Neocles, his adversary on the side of the **populace**.]

Some say, that [as boys], brought up together, they were ever contrary one to another in all their actions and doings, were it in sport, or in matters of earnest; and ever after, men began to see the natural inclination of them both, by their contrary affections. For Themistocles was quick, nimble, adventurous, and **subtle**, [engaging readily and eagerly in everything]. Aristides, contrariwise, was very quiet, temperate, constant, and marvellous well **staid**, who would for no respect be drawn away from equity and justice; neither would [he] lie, flatter, nor abuse anybody, though it were but in sport.

[omission for mature content; Plutarch says that the boys' youthful "heats and differences" carried on into their "public business" as adults]

In which calling, Themistocles sought the way to win friends, by whose means he came to great **preferment** in [a] short time, and [he] had made himself very strong by them. Therefore, when a friend of his told him one day [that] he was worthy to govern the city of Athens, and [would be] very fit for it, if he were **indifferent and not partial**; ["I wish," replied he, "I may never sit on that **tribunal** where my friends shall not plead a greater privilege than strangers."] But Aristides, taking another course by himself, would not **stand upon his friends** in government. First, because he would do no manner of wrong with pleasuring his friends; nor yet would [he cause them vexation] by denying their requests.

Secondly, because he saw many rulers and men of authority bold to do injustice, and manifest wrong, **bearing themselves upon their friends**; but he carried this opinion, that no honest man, or good citizen, should trust to any bolstering of friends, but to his own just and upright doings.

Notwithstanding, Aristides perceiving that Themistocles did rashly alter many things, and [**withstanding** and interrupting him in the whole series of his actions]; he was enforced sometime[s] to cross Themistocles again, and to speak against that [which] he preferred, partly to be even with him, but most[ly] to hinder his credit and authority, which increased still through the people's favour and good will towards him: thinking it better by contrarying him a little to disappoint sometime a thing that might have fallen out well for the commonwealth, rather than by [allowing] him to grow too great.

To conclude, it fortuned [once] that Themistocles having **preferred** a matter very profitable for the commonwealth, Aristides was so much against it [that] **Themistocles' purpose took no place**. Moreover, Aristides was so earnest against him, that when the council broke up after Themistocles' motion was rejected, he spoke it openly before them all: that the commonwealth of Athens would never prosper until they both were laid in Barathrum, which was a prison or hole wherein they put all thieves and condemned men.

Another time, Aristides moved a matter to the people, which divers were against. [He yet was **gaining the day**; but just as the president of the assembly was about to put it to the vote], Aristides perceiving by the arguments made against it that the matter he preferred was hurtful to the commonwealth, he gave it over, and would not have it pass. Many times also Aristides spoke by other men, when he would have a thing go forward; for fear lest Themistocles' spite towards him would hinder the benefit of the commonwealth.

They found him very constant and resolute in matters of state, whatsoever happened, which won him great **commendation**. For he was never the prouder for any honour they gave him, nor thought himself disgraced for any overthrow he received: being always of this mind, that it was the duty of an honest citizen to be ever ready to offer his body and life to do his country service, without respect and hope of reward of money, or for honour and glory. Therefore when certain verses were repeated in the theater, [in] one of the tragedies of Aeschylus, made in commendation of the ancient soothsayer Amphiaraus, to this effect:

> [For not at seeming just, but being so
>
> He aims; and from his depth of soil below

> Harvests of wise and prudent counsels grow,

the eyes of all the spectators turned on Aristides, as if this virtue, in an especial manner, belonged to him.]

Narration and Discussion

Why did Aristides worry that he and Themistocles could become too powerful? How did he try to prevent this?

Creative narration: The difference in personalities between Aristides and Themistocles could inspire a variety of imagined scenes or creative comparisons. One possibility might be to write brief school-type compositions telling what each boy wants to do when he grows up.

Lesson Three

Introduction

Part One continues the description of Aristides' justice and impartiality, not only to his friends but to his enemies.

Part Two tells, briefly, the story of the Battle of Marathon. Plutarch gives few details of the battle, for two reasons: first, it was a well-known story, and one he had told elsewhere; but, more importantly, his purpose in re-telling it here is to emphasize the character of Aristides, and to show how he earned the respect of the Athenians.

Vocabulary

plaint: charge

spoiled: looted

suborned: bribed, induced

through their practice they condemned him: they caused him to lose his position

carrying himself with more remissness: appearing to notice less of what was going on; acting with less diligence and attention

pillaged: robbed

dissembled: concealed his true feelings

bewrayed: revealed

ten captains: a change in the structure of Athenian government meant that the archon formerly responsible for the military had his duties taken over by a group of ten generals called **strategoi**

one hard by another: close to each other

archon eponymos: head magistrate of Athens; see introductory note

People

Darius: the king of Persia at that time

Miltiades: also called Miltiades the Younger; his family had been part of the rule of tyrants before the democratic reforms in Athens, but had been made to serve the Persians. He had taken part in a revolt against Persian rule, and had afterwards fled to Athens, but he was not initially trusted because of his history (and his political enemies continued to harass him throughout his life) However, his knowledge of Persian tactics played a large part in the victory at Marathon. Miltiades was the father of **Cimon** (see **Lesson Eleven**).

Historic Occasions

490 B.C.: Battle of Marathon

On the Map

Find a map showing the extent of the Persian empire at the time.

Attica is the area of Greece surrounding the city of **Athens**.

Reading

Part One

[He was a most determined champion for justice, not only against feelings of] favour and friendship, but hate and anger also. For in case of justice, neither could friendship make him go away for his friends' sake, nor [could] envy move him to do injustice to his very enemy.

For proof hereof it is written, that [when prosecuting the law against one who was his enemy], after the **plaint** was read, the judges were so angry with the offender that, without any more hearing of him, they would have given sentence against him. But Aristides, rising from his place, went and [knelt] at the judges' feet with the offender his enemy, and besought them to give him leave to speak, to justify and defend his cause, according to the course of the law.

Another time, he being judge between two private men that pleaded before him, one of them said unto him: "Aristides, this fellow, mine adversary here, hath done you great injury."

"My friend," quoth Aristides again, "I pray thee tell me only the injury he hath done *thee*, for I am here to do thee right, and not myself."

Moreover, he being chosen high treasurer of all the revenues of Athens, did declare that all the officers before him, [including] his late predecessors, had greatly robbed and **spoiled** the common treasure; but specially Themistocles:

["Well known he was an able man to be,

But with his fingers apt to be too free.]

Therefore when Aristides was to give up his account, Themistocles, and many other[s] **suborned** by him, were against him; and accused him [of] abusing his office; and followed him so hard that **through their practice they condemned him**, as Idomeneus writeth. Yet the noblest citizens, seeing what injury they offered Aristides, took his cause in hand, and found means to procure the people not only to release the fine imposed upon him, but to restore him again to his office of high treasurer for the year following. [Pretending now to repent him of his former practice, and **carrying himself with more remissness**, he became acceptable to such as **pillaged** the treasury, by not detecting or calling them to an exact account.] Whereupon such as were thieves and stealers of the treasure of the commonwealth did marvellously praise and like him; and became suitors for him to continue in the office.

But when the day of election came, that the Athenians would choose him again, Aristides [him]self reproved them, and said:

> "When I faithfully discharged the duty of mine
> office committed to me by you, I then received
> shame and reproach at your hands; and now that I
> have **dissembled**, not seeming to see the thefts
> and robberies done upon your treasure, ye [*brief
> omission*] say I am an honest man, and a good
> citizen. But I would you knew it, and I tell you
> plainly, I am more ashamed of the honour you do
> me now, than I was of the fine you did set upon me,
> when you condemned me the last year; and I am
> sorry to speak it, that you should think it more
> commendation to pleasure the wicked than to
> preserve the commonwealth."

After he had spoken these words and had **bewrayed** the common thefts the officers of the city did commit, he stopped the thieves' mouths that so highly praised and commended him for so honest a man; but yet of the noble and honest citizens he was much commended.

Part Two

Furthermore, on a time when Dathis, lieutenant to **Darius [the] king of Persia**, was come with all his navy to [land at] **Marathon**, in the country of **Attica**; upon pretense (as he said) to be revenged only of the Athenians that had burnt the city of Sardis, but indeed of [the] mind to conquer all Greece, and to destroy the whole country before him; the Athenians chose **ten captains** to go to the wars, among whom **Miltiades** was the chiefest man of authority.

But Aristides drew very near him in reputation and credit, because he did very good service in obtaining the victory, specially when he agreed with Miltiades in council to give battle upon the barbarous people; and also when he willingly gave Miltiades the whole rule and order of the army. For every one of the ten captains did by turns lead the whole army for one whole day; and when Aristides' turn came about, he gave his preferment thereof unto Miltiades, teaching his other companions that it was no shame, but [an] honour, for them to be ruled by the wisest. Thus, by his example, he appeased all strife that might have grown among them; and persuaded them all to be contented to follow his direction and counsel that had best experience in war. And so he did much advance Miltiades' honour. For after Aristides had once yielded his authority unto him, every one of the rest did the like when it came to their turn; and so they all submitted themselves unto his rule and leading.

But on the day of the battle, the place where the Athenians were [the hardest put to it] was in the midst of the battle, where they had set the tribes of the Leontides and of Antiochides: for thither the barbarous people did bend all their force, and made their greatest fight in that place. By which occasion, Themistocles and Aristides fighting **one hard by another** (for one was of the tribe Leontides, and the other of Antiochides), they valiantly fought it out with the enemies [*short omission*]. So, [with] the barbarous people at the last being overthrown, they made them flee, and drove them to their ships.

But when [the Persians] were embarked and gone, the captains of the Athenians, perceiving they made not towards the isles (which was their direct course to return into Asia), but that they were driven back by [the force of sea and wind] towards the coast of Attica, and the city of Athens, [the Greeks feared] they might find Athens unfurnished for defense, and might set upon it. They thereupon sent away presently nine tribes that marched thither with such speed as they came to Athens the very same day.

[Aristides, being left with his tribe at Marathon to guard the plunder and prisoners, did not disappoint the opinion they had of him.] For notwithstanding there was great store of gold and silver, much apparel, movables, and other infinite goods and riches in all their tents and pavilions, and in the ships also they had taken of theirs: he was not so covetous as once to touch them, nor to suffer any other to meddle with them (unless by stealth some provided for themselves).

[*short omission*]

Narration and Discussion

In Part One (and in the previous lessons), we see how Aristides carried out his duties in civil government and in the courts, and we may get an idea of him as an honest man but not one who would do particularly well in a physical setting such as a battlefield. In Part Two, though, that is exactly where we find him. How did the character traits he developed at home serve him again during the war against the Persians?

Lesson Four

Introduction

If you were a superhero, would you rather be known for might or virtue? Plutarch wonders why people throughout history seem to downplay virtue, "the only divine good really in our reach."

Vocabulary

divine: refers to gods or deities, divine beings

appellation, surname: an honourary name added to one's birth names

omnipotence: all-powerfulness

dissolute and licentious: prone to wild behaviour

ostracism: a ritual of banishment

specious, speciously: sounding true but not really so

mitigation: lessening, easing

base and villainous fellows: lower-class criminal sorts

desisted: stopped

a great shell: a **sherd**, a piece of broken pottery

Historic Occasions

489-488 B.C.: Aristides was **archon eponymos** (head magistrate)

485-482 B.C.: approximate dates of Aristides' ostracism

Reading

Part One

[Aristides, immediately after this, was chosen **archon [eponymos]**; although Demetrius the Phalerian says he held the office a little before he died after the Battle of Plataea.]

[*short omission giving evidence that Aristides was archon earlier, not later*]

[Of all his virtues, the common people were most affected with his justice, because of its continual and common use; and thus, although of mean fortune and ordinary birth, he possessed himself of the most kingly and **divine appellation** of "Just": which kings, however and tyrants have never sought after; but have taken delight to be **surnamed** besiegers of cities, thunderers, conquerors, or eagles again, and hawks; affecting, it seems, the reputation which proceeds from power and violence, rather than that of virtue.] And notwithstanding, God [Dryden: *the divinity*], whom men desire most to be likened to, doth excel all human nature in three special things: in immortality, in power, and in virtue; of which three, virtue is the most honourable and precious thing.

[*short omission*]

Therefore, because men commonly [give] three sundry honours to the gods: the first, that they think them blessed: the second, that they fear them: the third, that they reverence them: it appeareth then that they think them blessed for the eternity and immortality of their godhead; that they fear them because of their **omnipotence** and power; and that they love and worship them, for their justice and equity. And yet notwithstanding, of those three, men do covet immortality, which no flesh can attain unto; and also power, which dependeth most upon Fortune; and in the meantime they leave virtue alone, whereof the gods of their goodness have made us capable.

But here they shew themselves fools. For justice maketh the life of a noble man, and of one in great authority, seem divine and celestial: where, without justice, and dealing unjustly, his life is most beastly, and odious to the world.

Part Two

[Aristides, therefore, had at first the fortune to be beloved for this surname, but at length envied. Especially when Themistocles spread a rumour amongst the people that, by determining and judging all matters privately, he (Aristides)] had overthrown all justice, because by consent of the parties he was ever chosen arbitrator to end all controversies; and how by this means he secretly had procured the absolute power of a king, not needing any guard or soldiers about him.

The people moreover being grown very **dissolute and licentious**, by reason of the victory of Marathon, who sought that all things should pass by them, and their authority, began now to mislike, and to be greatly offended, that any private man should go before the rest in good fame and reputation. [Coming together, therefore, from all parts into the city, they banished Aristides by the **ostracism**, giving their jealousy of his reputation the name of fear of tyranny.]

[For ostracism was not the punishment of any criminal act; but was **speciously** said to be the mere depression and humiliation of excessive greatness and power; and was in fact a gentle relief and **mitigation** of envious feeling, which was thus allowed to vent itself in inflicting no intolerable injury, only a ten years' banishment. But after it came to be exercised upon **base and villainous fellows**, they **desisted** from it; Hyperbolus being the last whom they banished by the ostracism.]

[*omission for length: the story of Hyperbolus*]

[It was performed, to be short, in this manner.] At a certain day appointed, every citizen carried **a great shell** in his hand; whereupon he wrote the name of him he would have banished; and brought it into a certain place railed about with wooden bars in the marketplace. Then, when every man had brought in his shell, the magistrates and officers of the city did count and tell the number of them. (For if there were less than six thousand citizens that had thus brought these shells together: the [ostracism] was not full and perfect.) That done, they laid apart every man's name written in these shells; and whose name they found written by most citizens, they proclaimed him, by sound of trumpet, a banished man for ten years (during which time notwithstanding, the party did enjoy all his goods).

Now every man writing thus [the] name in a shell [of the one] whom they would have banished: it is reported there was a plain man of the country (very simple) that could neither write, nor read; who came to Aristides (being the first man he met with), and gave him his shell, praying him to write Aristides' name upon it.

[Aristides, being surprised], did ask the countryman if Aristides had ever done him any displeasure. "No," said the countryman, "he never did me hurt, nor I know him not: but [I am tired of hearing him everywhere called the Just]." Aristides, hearing him say so, gave him no answer, but wrote his own name upon the shell, and delivered it again to the countryman. But as he went his way out of the city, he lift[ed] up his hands to heaven, and made a prayer [*short omission*], beseeching the gods that the Athenians might never have such troubles in hand, as they should be compelled to call for Aristides again.

Narration and Discussion

How did Themistocles stir up the Athenians against Aristides?

If someone is "ostracized" now, it means that nobody will talk to him or work with him because he has done something shameful. How was Athenian thinking about ostracism quite different?

Creative narration: At an imaginary gathering of powerful leaders and rulers, each of whom wears a t-shirt with a logo and nickname (such as "The Mighty Eagle"); Aristides arrives with the simple words "The Just" on his shirt. What might be the reaction of the others? How might he still have the last word?

Lesson Five

Introduction

The **Battle of Salamis** was the victory of the Greek navy over the Persians, and that victory was world-changing. But Aristides wasn't there for the battle (he was handling matters at Psyttaleia); therefore Plutarch omits the details of how the Greeks trapped the large, unwieldy Persian ships in the narrow bay and sank enough of them to declare a victory. It is the hours leading up to the battle, the events on Psyttaleia, and the aftermath, that receive the focus.

Vocabulary

stratagem: plan of attack

approbation: approval

the keeping Asia (here) in Europe: keeping the Persian king from escaping back to his own country.

Lacedaemonians: Spartans

victuals: food

their city was burnt and razed: the Persians burned the Acropolis in Athens as well as other parts of the city

anathematize: curse; threaten with divine punishment

People

Xerxes, King of Persia: the successor to Darius

Eurybiades: a Spartan general who, at least officially, led the combined Greek forces.

Historic Occasions

480 B.C.: Battles of Thermopylae, Artemisium, and **Salamis**

480 B.C.: Aristides elected **Strategos (general)**

On the Map

Thessaly and Boeotia: regions or kingdoms in Greece

Salamis: an island near Athens

The **Hellespont** is the strait between the Aegean and the Sea of Marmara that separates Europe from Asia. It was the only route back to Persia.

Reading

Part One

Notwithstanding, within three years after, when **Xerxes, King of Persia** came with his army through the countries of **Thessaly and Boeotia**, and entered into the heart of the country of **Attica**: the Athenians [repealed the law and] called home again all those they had banished; and [e]specially, because they were afraid Aristides would take part with the barbarous people, and that his example should move many other[s] to do the like; wherein they were greatly deceived in the nature of the man. For before that he was called home, he continually travelled up and down, persuading and encouraging the Greeks to maintain and defend their liberty. [And afterwards, when Themistocles was general with absolute power, he assisted him in all ways both in action and counsel]; and thereby [he] won his enemy great honour, because it stood upon the safety and preservation of his country.

For when **Eurybiades** (the general of the army of the Greeks) had determined to forsake the **isle of Salamis**; and the galleys of the barbarous people were come into the midst of the seas, and had environed the isles all about, and the mouth of the arm of the **strait** of Salamis, before any man knew they were thus enclosed in: [Aristides, with great hazard, sailed from Aegina through the enemy's fleet]; and by good hap got in the night pinto Themistocles' tent, and calling him out, spoke with him there in this sort:

"Themistocles, if we be both wise, it is high time we

should now leave of this vain envy and spite we
[have] long time borne each other, and that we
should enter into another sort of envy more
honourable and profitable for us both. I mean,
which of us two should do his best endeavour to
save Greece: you [in the ruling and commanding];
and I, by counselling you for the best, and executing
your commandment; [even indeed, as I now
understand you to be alone adhering to the best
advice, in counselling without any delay to engage
in the straits. And in this, though our own party
oppose, the enemy seems to assist you.] For it is
said that the sea, both before and behind us and
round about us, is covered all over with their ships,
so as they that would not before, shall be now
compelled of force, and in spite of their hearts, to
fight and bestir them like men: because they are
compassed in all about, and there is no passage left
open for them to escape, nor to flee."

[To which Themistocles answered. "I would not willingly, Aristides, be overcome by you on this occasion; and shall endeavour, in emulation of this good beginning, to outdo it in my actions." Also relating to him the **stratagem** he had framed against the barbarians, he entreated him to persuade Eurybiades and show him how it was impossible they should save themselves without an engagement; as he was the more likely to be believed.

Whence, in the council of war, Cleocritus the Corinthian, telling Themistocles that Aristides did not like his advice, as he was present and said nothing, Aristides answered that he should not have held his peace if Themistocles had not been giving the best advice; and that he was now silent, not out of any good-will to the person, but in **approbation** of his counsel.

Thus the Greek captains were employed. But Aristides perceiving Psyttaleia, a small island that lies within the straits over against Salamis, to be filled by a body of the enemy; [he] put aboard his small boats the most forward and courageous of his countrymen, and went ashore upon it; and, joining battle with the barbarians, slew them all], taking the chiefest of them only prisoners; among which were three sons of Sandauce, the king's sister, whom he sent unto Themistocles.

[omission: the death of these three]

That done, Aristides dispersed his soldiers about the isle, to receive all such as were by fortune of war, or of the sea, cast into the island: to the end that no enemy of theirs should [e]scape their hands, nor any of his friends should perish. For the greatest fleet of all their ships, and the sharpest encounter of the whole battle, was about this little island; and therefore, the tokens of triumph were set there.

Part Two

After the battle was won, Themistocles, to feel Aristides' opinion, said unto him: "We have done a good piece of service, but yet there is another behind of greater importance, and that is this: **the keeping Asia (here) in Europe**, which we may easily do if we sail with all speed to the **strait of Hellespont**, and go break the bridge the king hath made there."

Then Aristides cried out, "Stay there, never speak of that: but I pray you, let us rather seek all the ways we can how to drive this barbarous king *out* of Greece; lest, if we keep him with so great an army and he shall see no way before him to escape out, we drive him then to fight like a desperate man, and peril ourselves we cannot tell to what."

[Omission for length: Themistocles sent word to Xerxes, by a Persian prisoner, that the Greeks wanted to destroy the bridge, but that they were being held off. The message was intended to send Xerxes into a panic, and it succeeded.]

King Xerxes being nettled [Dryden: *terrified*] with this advertisement, took straight his journey and with all speed went to recover the strait of Hellespont; and left **Mardonius** his lieutenant general in Greece, with three hundred thousand of the best soldiers of his army. This Mardonius was marvellously dreaded of all the Greeks, for the wonderful great army he had by land, and he did threaten them also by his letters he wrote unto them.

"You have," (said he) "with your ships by sea,
overcome men **acquainted** to fight by land, and
that never handled oars: but now, the plains of

> Thessaly, [and] the fields of Boeotia, are very fair
> and large for horsemen and **footmen** to make
> proof of their valiantness, if you will come to the
> battle in the field."

[But] he wrote letters to the Athenians, by the king his master's commandment, of other effect; and offered them, from him, to build up their city again, to give them a great pension, and furthermore to make them lords of all Greece, [if] they would give over, and leave off these wars. The **Lacedaemonians** being forthwith advertised of his letters written to the Athenians, and fearing lest they would have been persuaded by them, sent their ambassadors with all speed to Athens, to pray them to send their wives and children unto Sparta, and also to offer them **victuals**, to relieve their poor old people, because of the great scarcity that was at Athens; for **their city was burnt and razed**, and all their country besides destroyed by the barbarous people. The Athenians, having heard the offers of the ambassadors of Lacedaemon, made them a marvellous answer through Aristides' counsel, and this it was:

> That they bare with the barbarous people, though
> they [the Persians] thought all things were to be
> sold for gold and silver, because they esteemed
> nothing more precious, nor better in this world,
> than to be rich and wealthy; but on the other side,
> they were greatly offended with the
> Lacedaemonians, that they only regarded the
> present poverty and necessity of the Athenians, and
> did forget their virtue and noble courage, thinking
> to make them fight more valiantly for the
> preservation of Greece by offering them victuals to
> live withal.

The people approving this answer, Aristides then caused the ambassadors of Sparta to come to the assembly, and [he] commanded them to tell the Lacedaemonians by word of mouth, that all the gold above or under the ground could not corrupt the Athenians, to make them take any sum of money or reward, to leave the defense of the liberty of Greece. And to the herald that came from Mardonius, he showed him the sun, and said unto him: "So long as yonder sun keepeth his course about the world, so long will the Athenians be mortal enemies unto the Persians, because they have spoiled and destroyed all [our] country, and [have] defiled and burnt the temples of [our] gods." [Moreover, he proposed a decree that the priests should **anathematize** him who sent any herald to the Medes, or [who] deserted the alliance of Greece.]

Narration and Discussion

Why did the Athenians believe it was important to bring Aristides back from his banishment during the Persian attacks?

Why was Themistocles having a hard time getting his men to agree to fight in the straits? How did Aristides use his skills in conflict resolution during this time?

Why did the Athenians react so strongly to the seemingly generous offer of assistance from Sparta?

Creative narration: If Shakespeare had written a play about these events, how might he have dramatized the discussion between Themistocles and Aristides, and then the council of war?

Lesson Six

Introduction

In the **Battle of Plataea,** which took place the year after Salamis, Aristides led the Athenian forces, although **Pausanias** was the "head general."

Vocabulary

> **into the Isle of Salamis:** The Athenian leaders put the most vulnerable citizens out of harm's way by transporting them to the island
>
> **Ephori:** A group of five elected magistrates (judges) having supervisory power over the kings of Sparta.

sporting: "carelessly keeping holy day." The Ephori didn't want to appear too co-operative, so they insisted that they were in the middle of a festival and couldn't interrupt everything for some battle.

Helots: Spartan serfs (not exactly slaves, but not free citizens either)

bulwark: stockade, fortification

furlong: one-eighth of a mile

let the horsemen: keep the cavalry from getting up the hill

fane: temple, sacred place

frontiers: boundaries

contesting the post of honour: trying to take the top place

place neither giveth…: where you stand or fight is irrelevant

People

Pausanias: see introductory note

Historic Occasions

479 B.C.: Battle of Plataea

479 B.C.: Aristides re-elected Strategos (General)

On the Map

Plataea: a city in Boeotia (a region of central Greece).

Reading

Part One

Hereupon, when Mardonius came again the second time to overrun the country of Attica, the Athenians got them[selves] again **into the Isle of Salamis**; and then they sent Aristides [as] ambassador unto the

Lacedaemonians. He sharply took them up, and reproved their sloth and negligence, because they had again forsaken Athens, and left it to the spoil of the barbarous people: and prayed them yet they would look to save the rest of Greece.

The **Ephori** (which were certain officers that ruled all things within the city of Sparta), [made show of **sporting** all day, and of carelessly keeping [a] holy day (for they were then celebrating the Hyacinthian festival); but in the night, selecting five thousand Spartans, each of whom was attended by seven **Helots**, they sent them forth, unknown to those from Athens. And when] Aristides came again into their council, to complain of their negligence, they fell a-laughing, and said he dreamed, or else he mocked them: for their army which they had sent against "the strangers" (for so they called the Persians) was already at the city of Orestion in Arcadia. Aristides, hearing their answer, replied that they were to blame, to mock them in that sort, to send away their men so secretly that they might not know of it; and that it was no time for them now to go about to deceive their friends, but their enemies rather. Idomeneus in his story reporteth the matter thus in every point. [But in the decree of Aristides, not himself, but Cimon, Xanthippus, and Myronides are appointed ambassadors.]

Part Two

[Being chosen [Athenian] general for the war, Aristides] went unto the camp of the Greeks by the city of **Plataea**, with eight thousand footmen well armed and appointed. There he found **Pausanias**, the "generalissimo" [*Dryden*] of all the whole power and army of the Greeks, who brought with him the force of Sparta; and there came daily into his camp, one after another, a marvellous great multitude of other Greeks.

Now touching the army of the barbarous people, they encamped all alongst the River Asopus; but because their camp stretched out a marvellous way in length, they were not [enclosed] at all; [but their baggage and most valuable things were surrounded with a square **bulwark**, each side of which was the length of ten **furlongs**].

*[Omission for length: the Greeks prayed and made sacrifices to predict the outcome of the battle. They consulted the **oracle** at Delphi, which seemed to say*

that they should fight in a place called Ceres Eleusina, some distance away. Then the captain of the Plataeans had a dream that "Eleusis" referred to a spot within their own territory.]

Arimnestus having seen this vision in his sleep; when he did awake in the morning, he straight sent for the oldest citizens, and considering with them where this place should be, he found, at the length, that at the foot of Mount Cithaeron, by the city of Nysia, there was an old temple they called the "Temple of Ceres Eleusinia and Proserpine." When he heard them say so, he went straight and told Aristides of it, and found that it was an excellent place to set an army in battle array that had but few horsemen: for that the foot of Mount Cithaeron did **let the horsemen**, they could not go to the place where the temple stood, and where the plain and valley did end. [Also, in the same place, there was the **fane** of Androcrates, environed with a thick shady grove. And that the oracle might be accomplished in all particulars for the hope of victory, Arimnestus proposed, and the Plataeans decreed, that the **frontiers** of their country towards Attica should be removed, and the land given to the Athenians, that they might fight in defense of Greece in their own proper territory.]

This noble gift and present of the Plataeans was so famous, as many years after, King Alexander the Great, having conquered the Empire of Asia, built up the walls again of the city of Plataea; and when he had done, [he] made a herald openly proclaim it at the Games Olympical: that Alexander had done the Plataeans that honour and dignity for a memorial and honour of their magnanimity. Because in the war against the Persians, they had freely and liberally given away their land unto the Athenians, for the safety of [all] the Greeks: and had showed themselves of a noble courage also, and very willing to defend the state of Greece.

Part Three

[The Tegeatans, **contesting the post of honour** with the Athenians, demanded that, according to custom, the Lacedaemonians being ranged on the right wing of the battle, they might have the left, alleging several matters in commendation of their ancestors.] But Aristides stepped between them [*the Tegeatans and the Athenians*] and told them [*the Athenians*] that it was no time now to contend with the Tegeatans about their nobility and valiantness.

> "And as for you, my Lords of Sparta," said he, "and you also, my masters of Greece: we tell you, that **place neither giveth nor taketh virtue away**, and we do assure you that wheresoever you place us, we will so defend and keep it, as we will not impair nor blemish the honour we have won in former[ly] fought battles, and gotten victories. For we are not come hither to quarrel and fall out with our friends, but to fight with our common enemies: nor to brag of our ancestors' doings, but to show ourselves valiant in defense of all Greece. [This battle will manifest how much each city, captain, and private soldier is worth to Greece.]"

When Aristides had spoken, the captains and all other of the council concluded in favour of the Athenians, that they should have one of the wings of the battle.

Narration and Discussion

Based on the previous lesson, does it seem fair for Aristides to have scolded the Spartans for not helping Athens? What might explain this change of attitude? Why did the Spartans send their troops off in secret?

Show how Aristides modelled wisdom, tact, and the ability to handle people's egos and keep the peace.

Lesson Seven

Introduction

The mood of the Athenians, especially the formerly wealthy ones who had lost political status as well as material goods, was at a low point. Aristides discovered that some of them were conspiring to overthrow the Athenian government; or, if they failed, to surrender the city to the Persians. It would normally have pleased Aristides' sense of justice to have traitors exposed and swiftly dealt with. However, he was wise enough to see that there was an even greater issue at stake.

Vocabulary

discountenanced: having lost status ("lost face")

preferred: promoted

came to an inkling of it: heard about it

because of the time: because this was such a critical time

public convenience: the benefit of the people

apprehended: arrested

whom they would have indicted as principals: whom they would have accused of leading the conspiracy

emulation in valour: ambition to show their bravery

backward: hesitant or unwilling

visor: headpiece

victuals waxed scant: they were running out of food

continual repair to their camp: Greek soldiers continued to arrive

People

Alexander, King of Macedon: this was **Alexander I**, whose kingdom was subject to Persia. He was known, as in this story, for his sympathy towards Greece

On the Map

Mount Cithaeron: a mountain range about ten miles long, in central Greece, which forms the northern boundary of the region of Attica

Reading

Part One

[All Greece being in suspense, and especially the affairs of the Athenians unsettled, certain persons of great families and possessions having been impoverished by the war], and seeing themselves **discountenanced**, not bearing that rule and authority in the commonwealth they were wont to do, because other[s] were called to authority, and **preferred** to the offices of the city: they gathered together and met at a house in the city of Plataea, and there [they] conspired to overthrow the authority of the people at Athens [*Dryden: the democratic government*]; and if they could not obtain their purpose, then that they would rather lose all, and betray their country unto the barbarous people.

While these things were practised in the camp, many being of the conspiracy, Aristides **came to an inkling of it**, and was marvellously afraid, **because of the time**: wherefore he began to be careful of the matter, being of such importance as it was, and yet [he did not wish to expose] the whole conspiracy, little knowing what a number might be drawn into this treason, if it were narrowly looked into; he was [willing to set bounds to his justice with a view to the **public convenience**].

So he caused eight persons only of the great number to be **apprehended**; and of these eight, the two first **whom they would have indicted as principals** and [who] were most to be burdened for the conspiracy, Aeschines of the town of Lampra, and Agesias of the town of Acharnae, they found means to flee out of the camp, and to save themselves. [The rest he dismissed; giving opportunity to such as thought themselves concealed to take courage and repent]; saying that the battle should be their judge, where they should purge themselves of all accusations laid against them, and show the world also, that they never had any other intention but honest[y] and good towards their country.

Part Two

Mardonius, to prove the courage of the Greeks, had sent all his horsemen (wherein he was far stronger than the Greeks) to skirmish with them. [The Greeks] were lodged at the foot of **Mount Cithaeron**, in strong places and full of stones, saving the three thousand Megarians, that camped in the plain: by reason whereof, they were sore troubled and hurt by the horsemen of the barbarous people that set upon them on every side, for they might charge them where they would. Insomuch, in the end, perceiving they alone could no longer resist the force of so great a multitude of the barbarous people, they sent with all speed possible to Pausanias, to pray him to send them present aid.

Pausanias, hearing this news, and seeing in his own sight the camp of the Megarians almost all covered with shot and darts which the barbarous people threw at them, and that they were compelled to stand close together in a little corner: he [knew] not what to do. For to go thither in person with the Lacedaemonians, that were footmen heavy armed, he thought that was no way to help them. [He proposed it, therefore, as a point of **emulation in valour** and love of distinction, to the commanders and captains who were around him, if any would voluntarily take upon them the defense and succour of the Megarians. The rest being **backward**, Aristides undertook the enterprise for the Athenians]; and brought **Olympiodorus** into the field, (one of the valiantest captains that served under him), with his company of three hundred chosen men, and certain [archers] mingled amongst them. These soldiers were ready in a moment, and marched straight in battle [ar]ray, [at] a great pace towards the barbarous people.

Masistius, that was general of the horsemen of the Persians, a goodly tall man, perceiving their coming towards him: turned his horse, and galloped to them. The Athenians tarried him, and kept their ground, and the encounter was very hot, because both the one and the other side did the best they could at this first onset to put the rest of the battle in jeopardy: and they fought so long, that Masistius' horse was shot through the body with an arrow [and flung him, and he falling could hardly raise himself through the weight of his armour]; as for that the Athenians came so suddenly upon him. [The Athenians, pressing upon him with blows], could find no way to kill him, he was so thoroughly armed and laden with gold, copper, and iron, not only upon his body and his head, but also on his legs and arms: until at the length there was one that thrust the head of his dart through his [**visor**], and so killed him. The Persians perceiving that, fled immediately, and forsook the body of their general.

[omission for length]

Part Three

After this first skirmish, both the one and the other side kept their camp, and would not come into the field many days after: for the soothsayers did promise both sides the victory, as much the Persians, as the Greeks, [if] they did but only defend: and contrarywise, they did threaten them to be overthrown that did assault.

But Mardonius finding **victuals waxed scant**, and that they were stored but for few days, and moreover how the Greeks daily grew stronger by **continual repair to their camp**, the longer he delayed; in the end he resolved to tarry no longer, but to pass the river of Asopus the next morning by break of day, and suddenly to set upon the Greeks. So he gave the captains warning the night before what they should do, because every man should be ready. But about midnight there came a horseman [who stole into the Greek camp, and, coming to the watch], told them he would speak with Aristides, general of the Athenians. Aristides was called for straight, and when he came to him, the horseman said unto Aristides:

> "I am **Alexander, King of Macedon**, [and I am
> arrived here through the greatest danger in the
> world for the goodwill I bear you, lest a sudden
> onset should dismay you, so as to behave in the
> fight worse than usual. For tomorrow Mardonius
> will give you battle, urged not by any hope of
> success or courage, but by want of victuals; since,
> indeed, the prophets prohibit him the battle, the
> sacrifices and oracles being unfavourable]; which
> hath put all the army in a marvellous fear, and
> [they] stand in no good hope at all. Thus he is
> forced to put all at adventure; or else if he will needs
> lie still, to be starved to death for very famine."

After King Alexander had imparted this secret to Aristides, he prayed him to keep it to himself, and to remember it in time to come. Aristides answered him then, that it was no reason he should keep a matter of so great importance as that, from Pausanias, who was their lieutenant general of the whole army: notwithstanding, he promised him he would tell it no man else before the battle, and that if the gods gave the Greeks the victory, he did assure him they should all acknowledge his great favour and good will showed unto them. After they had talked thus together, King Alexander left him, and returned back again: and Aristides also went immediately to Pausanias' tent, and told him the talk King Alexander and he had together. Thereupon, the private captains were sent for straight to council, and the order was given that every man should have his bands ready, for they should fight in the morning.

Narration and Discussion

Why was Aristides willing to delay his own inclination to get to the bottom of the conspiracy and punish all those involved? Was that a good decision in this case?

Why did King Alexander come at night to warn the Greeks of the impending attack?

Creative narration: Write a letter or a diary entry as one of the conspirators who was shown grace by Aristides. Would you be grateful for this second chance, or angry that the rebellion did not happen as planned?

Lesson Eight

Introduction

After the Greek troops shuffled their positions, the Persians responded by moving their soldiers around in the same way. The back-and-forth continued for a good part of the day, but without any fighting. Then the Greeks decided that they needed to camp in a place with better water supplies, so they began to move things around even more; but this was misinterpreted as an order to retreat, and the frustrated soldiers responded with something close to a mutiny. Was there any hope at all of success?

Vocabulary

so much the lustier: more vigorously

their natural countrymen anciently descended of them: those of Greek descent who were fighting on the Persian side

sundry: various

the order of their battle: the arrangement of their troops

dispersing: scattering

suffrage: vote

in trifling thus: while wasting time in this way

the Greeks did forsake…: the Greeks had moved camp

People

Herodotus: historian famous for his account of the Persian wars

Thebans: the Thebans were Greeks, but they were fighting on the Persian side

Reading

Part One

So Pausanias at that time (as **Herodotu**s writeth) said unto Aristides that he would remove the Athenians from the left to the right wing, because they should have the Persians themselves right before them, and that they should fight **so much the lustier**, both for that they were acquainted with their [way of combat], as also because they had overcome them before in the first encounter; and that [he] himself would take the left wing of the battle, where he should encounter with the Greeks that fought on the Persians' side. But when all the other private captains of the Athenians understood it, they were marvellous angry with Pausanias, and said he did them wrong, and had no reason to let all the other Greeks keep their place where they were always appointed, and only to remove them, as if they were slaves, to be appointed at his pleasure, now of one side, then of the other, and to set them to fight with the valiantest soldiers they had of all their enemies.

Then said Aristides to them, that they knew not what they said; and [he reminded them] how before they misliked, and did strive with the Tegeatans (**Lesson Six**), only for having the left wing of the battle; and when it was granted, they thought themselves greatly honoured that they were preferred before them, by order of the captains; and now where the Lacedaemonians were willing of themselves to give them the place of the right wing, and did in manner offer them the pre-eminence of the whole army, they do not thankfully take the honour offered them, nor yet do reckon of the [ad]vantage and benefit given them to fight against the Persians [them]selves, their ancient enemies, and not against **their natural countrymen anciently descended of them**.

When Aristides had used all these persuasions unto them, they were very well contented to change place with the Lacedaemonians: and then all the talk among them was to encourage one another, and to tell them that the Persians that came against them had no better hearts, nor weapons, than those whom they before had overcome in the plain of Marathon.

> "For," said they, "they have the same [bows and
> arrows, and the same embroidered coats and gold],
> hanging on their cowardly bodies and faint hearts;
> where we have also the same weapons and bodies
> we had, and our hearts more lively and courageous
> than before, through the **sundry** victories we have
> since gotten of them. Further, we have this
> advantage more: that we do not fight as our other
> confederates the Greeks do, for our city and country
> only; but also to continue the fame and renown of
> our former noble service, which we won at the
> battles of Marathon and of Salamis: to the end the
> world should not think that the glory of these
> triumphs and victories was due unto Miltiades only,
> or unto fortune, but unto the courage and
> worthiness of the Athenians."

Thus were the Greeks thoroughly occupied to change **the order of their battle** in haste. [But the **Thebans**, understanding it by some deserters, forthwith acquainted Mardonius; and he, either for fear of the Athenians, or of a desire to engage the Lacedaemonians, marched over his Persians to the other wing, and commanded the Greeks of his party to be posted opposite to the Athenians.] This alteration was so openly done, that every man might see it: whereupon Pausanias removed the Lacedaemonians again, and set them in the right wing. Mardonius, seeing that, removed the Persians again from the left wing, and brought them to the right wing (where they were before) against the Lacedaemonians; and thus they consumed all that day in changing their men to and fro.

Part Two

So the captains of the Greeks sat in council at night; and there they agreed that they must needs remove their camp, and lodge in some other place where they might have water at commandment: because their enemies did continually trouble and spoil that water they had about them, with their horses.

Now when night came, the captains would have marched away with their men, to go to the lodging they had appointed: but the [soldiers] went very ill-willing to it, and [the captains] had much ado to keep them together. For they were no sooner out of the trenches and fortification of their camp, but the most part of them ran to the city of Plataea, and were marvellously out of order, **dispersing** themselves here and there, and set up their tents where they thought good, before the places were appointed for them; and there were none that tarried behind but the Lacedaemonians only, and that was against their wills. For one of their captains, called Amompharetus, a marvellous hardy man that feared no danger, and longed sore for battle: he was in such a rage with these trifling delays, that he cried it out in the camp, that this removing was a goodly running away, and [protested he would not desert his post], but would there tarry Mardonius' coming with his company.

Pausanias went to him and told him he must do that [which] the other Greeks had consented to in council by [the] most voices. But Amompharetus took a great stone in his hands, and threw it down at Pausanias' feet, and told him, "[By this token do I give my **suffrage** for the battle; nor have I any concern with the cowardly consultations and decrees of other men.]"

Amompharetus' stubbornness did so amaze Pausanias that he was at his wit's end. So he sent unto the Athenians that were onwards on their way, [to stay to accompany him; and so he himself set off with the rest of the army for Plataea, hoping thus to make Amompharetus move.]

But **in trifling thus**, the day brake: and Mardonius understanding that **the Greeks did forsake their first lodging**, he made his army presently march in battle [ar]ray to set upon the Lacedaemonians.

Narration and Discussion

How did Aristides persuade the Athenians that they were wrong to complain about fighting opposite the Persians? After they agreed to the change, what did they expect to happen next? What events interfered?

Creative narration: Speak or write as an on-the-spot reporter, or as someone present at the battle. What would you predict as the outcome of the battle, from the situation as it currently appears? What are the greatest obstacles to a Greek victory?

Lesson Nine

Introduction

Errors in communication, along with other mistakes, seemed disastrous for the Greeks, and particularly for the Lacedaemonians who were left behind at the original camp. Pausanias, in a panicked state of mind, did not organize a defense; but simply ordered his men to stand their ground while he went off to pray.

Vocabulary

expiring: dying

wonderful: something to wonder at (but not necessarily something good)

bestowed their arrows lustily: shot their arrows with great force

overthwart: across

scimitar: a short sword with a curved blade

conjured: commanded

the multitude: the common people

Reading

Part One

So the barbarous people made great shouts and cries, [as if they were not about to join battle, but crush the Greeks in their flight. Which within a very little came to pass.] For Pausanias, seeing the countenance of his enemies, made his ensigns to stay, and commanded every man to prepare to fight: but he forgot to give the [other] Greeks the signal of the battle, either for the anger he took against Amompharetus, or for the sudden onset of the enemies; which [meant] that they came not in [immediately or in a body to their assistance], but straggling in small companies, some here and some there.

[Pausanias, offering sacrifice, could not procure favourable omens]; so he commanded the Spartans to throw their targets at their feet, and not to stir out of their places, but only to do as he bade them, without resisting their enemies. When he had given this straight order, he went again and did sacrifice, when the horsemen of the enemies were at hand, and that their arrow[s] flew amongst the thickest of the Lacedaemonians, and did hurt divers of them, and [e]specially poor Callicrates among the rest, that was one of the goodliest men in all the army. [He, being shot with an arrow and upon the point of **expiring**, said that he lamented not his death (for he came from home to lay down his life in the defense of Greece)]; but it grieved him to die so cowardly, having given the enemy never a blow. His death was marvellous lamentable, and the constancy of the Spartans **wonderful:** [for they let the enemy charge without repelling them; and, expecting their proper opportunity from the gods and their general, suffered themselves to be wounded and slain in their ranks.]

[*short omission*]

Then was Pausanias in great distress to see the priests offer sacrifice upon sacrifice, and that not one of them pleased the gods: at the last he turned his eyes to the temple of Juno, and wept, and holding up his hands, besought Juno [of] Cithaeron, and all the other gods (patrons and protectors of the country of the Plataeans), that if it were not the will of the gods the Greeks should have the victory, yet that the conquerors at the least should buy their deaths dearly, and that they should find they fought against valiant men and worthy soldiers.

Part Two

Pausanias had no sooner ended his prayer, but the sacrifices fell out very favourable; insomuch the priests and soothsayers came to promise him victory. [The word being given, the Lacedaemonian battalion of foot seemed, on the sudden, like some one fierce animal, setting up his bristles, and betaking himself to the combat; and the barbarians perceived that they encountered with men who would fight it to the death.] Wherefore they covered their bodies with great targets, after the Persian fashion, and **bestowed their arrows lustily** upon the Lacedaemonians. But they, keeping close together and covering themselves with their shields, marched on still upon them, until they came to join with the enemy so lustily that they made their targets fly out of their hands, with the terrible thrusts and blows of their pikes and spears upon their breasts, and **overthwart** their faces, [so] that they slew many of them, and laid them on the ground.

For all that, they died not cowardly, but took the Lacedaemonians' pikes and spears in their bare hands, and broke them in two by strength of their arms: and then they quickly plucked out their **scimitars** and axes, and lustily laid about them, and wrung the Lacedaemonians' shields out of their hands by force, and fought it out with them a great while, hand to hand.

Part Three

Now, whilst the Lacedaemonians were busily fighting with the barbarous people, the Athenians stood still embattled far off, and kept their ground. But when they saw the Lacedaemonians tarry so long, and that they came not, and heard a marvellous noise of men as though they were fighting; and besides that there came a speedy messenger unto them sent from Pausanias, to let them understand they were fighting; then they marched with all speed they could to help them.

But as they were coming on [at] a great pace over the plain, unto that part where they heard the noise: the Greeks that were on Mardonius' side came against them. Aristides, seeing them coming towards them, went a good way before his company, and cried out as loud as he could for life, and **conjured** the Greeks in the name of the gods, the protectors of Greece, to leave off these wars, [and be no impediment or stop to those who were going to succour the defenders of Greece]. But when he saw [they would give no attention to him, and had prepared themselves for the battle; then turning from the present relief of the Lacedaemonians, he engaged them, being five thousand in number. But the greatest part soon gave way and retreated, as the barbarians also were put to flight.] The fury of the battle, and cruelest fight (as they say) was where the Thebans were: because the nobility and chiefest men of the country fought very earnestly for the Persians, but **the [multitude]** refused, being led by a small number of the nobility that commanded them.

Narration and Discussion

Based on the beating that the Lacedaemonians took at the beginning of the passage, the chances of success for the Greeks seemed slim. But suddenly the wind seemed to change, and "the barbarians were put to flight." How might the Greeks have accounted for this? Are there any other possible explanations?

Lesson Ten

Introduction

The battle was over; the Persians were defeated; but which of the Greek states deserved the greatest credit and honour? (Would they have to fight over it?)

Vocabulary

palisade: fort

give place unto: give first place to (and take second place behind)

suffer: allow

stayed: kept them from acting

requisite: necessary

fell out: quarreled

contention: disagreement

temple of Apollo Pythias: the temple at Delphi

levy: gather

People

Thebans: see **Lesson Eight**

the Greeks that fled: the Thebans

Minerva: Roman name for Athena, the goddess of war

On the Map

It might be interesting to measure the distance between **Delphi** and **Plataea**. Is it surprising that the runner dropped dead upon arrival?

Reading

Part One

So they fought that day in two places, the Lacedaemonians being the first that overthrew the Persians, and made them flee; and they slew Mardonius, the king's lieutenant, with a blow of a stone [that] one Arimnestus, a Spartan, gave him upon his head.

[*short omission*]

They drove the fliers within their walls of wood; and, a little time after, the Athenians put the **Thebans** to flight, killing three hundred of the chiefest and of greatest note among them in the actual fight itself. [For when they began to flee, news came that the army of the barbarians was besieged within their **palisade**; and so giving the Greeks opportunity to save themselves, they marched to assist at the fortifications; and coming in to the Lacedaemonians, who were altogether unhandy and inexperienced in storming, they took the camp with great slaughter of the enemy.] For of three hundred thousand, forty thousand only are said to have escaped with Artabasus; while on the Greeks' side there perished in all thirteen hundred and sixty; [of which fifty-two were Athenians, all of the tribe Æantis, that fought, says Clidemus, with the greatest courage of any].

[*omission for length*]

Part Two

After this great battle and overthrow of the barbarous people, there rose great strife betwixt the Athenians and the Lacedaemonians, touching the reward and honour of the victory. For the Athenians would not **give place unto** the Lacedaemonians, nor **suffer** them to set up any tokens or signs of triumph. Whereupon the Greeks running to arms in mutiny together, by this occasion they [would have] almost spoiled one another, had not Aristides, through his wisdom and wise persuasions, **stayed** and quieted the other captains, his companions; [e]specially Leocrates and Myronides, whom he [pacified and persuaded to leave the thing to the decision of the Greeks. And on their proceeding to discuss the matter,] Theogiton, a captain of the Megarians, said, for his opinion, that to avoid the civil war [which] might grow between the Greeks upon this quarrel, he thought it very **requisite** to appoint over the reward and honour of this victory unto some other city, than to any of the two that **fell out** about it.

After him rose up Cleocritus [the] Corinthian. [It seemed] to every man there that he would have requested this honour for the city of Corinth, [it] being indeed the third city in estimation of all Greece, next unto Sparta and Athens; howbeit he made an oration in commendation of the Plataeans, which was marvellously liked, and well thought of [by] every man. For his opinion went [in favour of the Plataeans; and counselled to take away all **contention** by giving them the reward and glory of the victory, whose being honoured could be distasteful to neither party.] Upon his words, Aristides first agreed on the Athenians' behalf, and then Pausanias for the Lacedaemonians, that the Plataeans should have the reward.

Now they both being agreed, before the spoil was divided between them, they set aside fourscore talents that were given to the Plataeans, with the which they built a temple unto **Minerva**, and gave her an image, and set out all her temple with pictures that remain whole until this day; and the Lacedaemonians notwithstanding did set up their tokens of victory by themselves, and the Athenians theirs also by themselves. So, they sending unto the oracle of Apollo in the city of Delphi, to know unto what gods and how they should do sacrifice: Apollo answered them that they should build up an altar unto Jupiter, protector of their liberty; howbeit that they should put no sacrifice upon it until they had first [extinguished the fires throughout the country, as having been defiled by the barbarians, and had kindled unpolluted fire at the common altar at Delphi.]

This answer being delivered, the great lords and officers of Greece went through all the country, to put out the fire[s] everywhere. And there was a man of the same city of Plataea at that time called Euchidas, that came and offered himself, and promised he would bring them fire from the **temple of Apollo Pythias**, with all possible speed that might be. So when he came to the city of Delphi, after he had sprinkled and purified his body with clean water, he put a crown of laurel upon his head, and went in that manner to take fire from the altar of Apollo.

When he had done, he hied him again as fast as he could run for life, into the city of Plataea, and came thither before the sun was set, having come and gone that day a thousand furlongs. But after he had saluted his citizens and delivered them the fire he brought: he fell down dead at their feet, and gave up the ghost. [But the Plataeans, taking him up, interred him in the temple of Diana Euclia, setting this inscription over him]:

> Engraved here doth lie, Euchidas speedy man,
>
> Who in one day, both to and fro, to Delphi lightly
> ran.

[*omission*]

Part Three

Afterwards there was a general council [held] by all the Greeks, in the which Aristides made a motion that all the cities of Greece should yearly send their deputies at a certain day appointed, unto the city of Plataea, there to make their prayers and sacrifices unto the gods; and that [every fifth year] they should celebrate common games, that should be called the Games of Liberty; and that they should also **levy** through all the provinces of Greece, for maintenance of the wars against the Persians and barbarous people, ten thousand footmen, a thousand horsemen, and a fleet of a hundred sail; [but the Plataeans [were] to be exempt, and sacred to the service of the gods, offering sacrifice for the welfare of Greece.] All which articles were enacted in [the] form and manner aforesaid; and the Plataeans bound themselves yearly to keep solemn sacrifices and anniversaries for the souls of the Greeks that were slain in their territories, fighting for defense of the liberty of the Greeks. And this they observe yet unto this day.

[*omission for length: details of the memorial procession*]

Narration and Discussion

Why was it so important to name one of the city-states as the chief victor over the Persians? What part did Aristides play in that decision?

Creative narration: Report (dramatically or in writing) on the events of the battle, and of the plans to commemorate the victory.

Lesson Eleven

Introduction

The Wars were over, but the large egos of various leaders (particularly Pausanias) were causing trouble in Greece. Could the states ever work together, and who could manage them without being sidetracked by personal ambition?

Vocabulary

popular state: one run with a democratic government

yet in arms, and very stout: well-armed and strong

for diverse respects: for various reasons

withal: at the same time

the tyranny and selfishness of Pausanias: see introductory notes

to command the other people of Greece: this refers to the formation of the Delian League, an alliance of Greek city-states

constrained: forced

manifest: clear, plain

hold their hands: stop them from acting

rated: taxed

indifferently: all alike, impartially

throw the perjury upon him: put the blame on him

convenience: necessity and the benefit of the commonwealth

People

Cimon: an Athenian statesman and military hero

Historic Occasions

478 B.C.: Formation of the Delian League

Reading

Part One

Now when the Athenians were returned to Athens, Aristides perceiving the people were bent to [e]stablish a **popular state**, where the people might bear the whole rule and authority, judging them well worthy to be considered of [this], in respect of their noble service and valiant courage they had showed in this war; and considering also that they would hardly be brought to like of any other government, being **yet in arms, and very stout**, by reason of the famous victories they had obtained. [He brought forward a decree that everyone might share in the government and the archons be chosen out of the whole body of the Athenians.]

And moreover, when Themistocles told, in open assembly, that he had a thing in his head [which] would be greatly to the profit and commodity of the state, but yet it was not to be spoken openly **for diverse respects**: the people willed him to tell it unto Aristides only, and to take his advice in it, to know whether it was meet to be done or not.

Then Themistocles told him secretly between them, that he thought to set the arsenal afire where all the [other] Greeks' ships lay: alleging that by this means the Athenians should be the greatest men of power in all Greece. Aristides hearing that, without any more, came presently to the people again, and told the whole council openly that nothing could be more profitable indeed for the whole commonwealth, and **withal** more wicked and unjust, than that [which] Themistocles thought good to do. When the people heard Aristides' answer, they willed Themistocles to let his device alone whatsoever it were: so great justicers were the Athenians, and so much did they trust Aristides' wisdom and equity besides.

Part Two

[Being sent in joint commission with **Cimon** to the war, he took notice that Pausanias and the other Spartan captains made themselves offensive by imperiousness and harshness to the confederates; and by being himself gentle and considerate with them, and by the courtesy and disinterested temper which Cimon, after his example, manifested in the expeditions, he stole away the chief command from the Lacedaemonians, neither by weapons, ships, or horses, but by equity and wise policy. For the Athenians being endeared to the Greeks by the justice of Aristides and by Cimon's moderation, **the tyranny and selfishness of Pausanias** rendered them yet more desirable.]

[*omission: the harsh treatment of Pausanias towards his men, and his arrogance towards Aristides*]

Whereupon the captains of the other Greeks, and specially those of Chios, of Samos, and of Lesbos, did afterwards follow Aristides, and persuaded him to take upon him the charge and authority **to command the other people of Greece**, and to take into his protection the allies and confederates of the same, who long [since had] wished to revolt from the government of the Lacedaemonians, and only [wished] to submit themselves unto the Athenians. Aristides answered them thus:

> "that they had not only reason to do that [which]
> they said, but that they were also **constrained** to
> do it. Notwithstanding, because the Athenians
> might have good ground and assurance of their
> undoubted fidelity and good service, they [the other
> cities] should deliver them **manifest** testimony and
> assurance thereof, by some famous act attempted
> against the Lacedaemonians, whereby their people
> hereafter durst never fall from the league of the
> Athenians."

[Upon which Uliades, the Samian, and Antagoras of Chios, conspiring together, ran in near Byzantium on Pausanias' galley, getting her between them as she was sailing before the rest.] Pausanias, seeing them, stood up straight in a marvellous rage against them, and threatened them that before it were long he would make them know they had been better to have assaulted their own natural country, than to have set upon him as they had done.

But they answered him, and bade him get him away quickly [if] he were wise, and let him thank Fortune hardly, that granted the Greeks victory at the Battle of Plataea under his leading: and that it was nothing else but only reverence and respect of the same, that had made the Greeks **hold their hands** till now from giving him that just punishment [which] his pride and arrogancy had deserved. So the end was, they left the Lacedaemonians, and stuck unto the Athenians: wherein was easily discerned the great courage and wonderful magnanimity of the Lacedaemonians. For when they saw their captains were marred and corrupted, through the over-great authority and liberty they had, they willingly gave up their commandment over the other Greeks, and did no more send their captains to be generals of the whole army of Greece: thinking it better for their citizens, that they should be obedient, and in every point observe the discipline and law of their country, than if they had been otherwise the only rulers and lords over the whole country.

[Even during the command of the Lacedaemonians, the Greeks [had] paid a certain contribution towards the maintenance of the war; and [now] being desirous to be **rated** city by city in their due proportion], they prayed the Athenians they would appoint Aristides to take order for it, unto whom they gave full power and authority to tax and [assess] every city **indifferently**, considering the greatness of the territory, and the revenues of the same, as everyone was reasonably able to bear it.

[omission for length about Aristides' high rate of taxation over the confederacy, which seems to have been well-accepted rather than detested]

Part Three

[Aristides, therefore, having acquired a wonderful and great reputation by this levy of the tribute, Themistocles is said to have derided him, as if this had been not the commendation of a man, but a money-bag; a retaliation, though not in the same kind, for some free words which Aristides had used. For when Themistocles once was saying that he thought the highest virtue of a general was to understand and foreknow the measures the enemy would take], Aristides replied, "And so is it not only a needful, but an honest thing, and meet for a worthy general of an army, to be clean-fingered, without bribery or corruption."

So Aristides made all the other people of Greece to swear that they would truly keep the articles of the alliance; and he himself, as general of the Athenians, [took the oath] in the name of the Athenians; and so pronouncing execrations and curses against them that should break the league and oath taken, he threw iron wedges red hot into the sea, and prayed the gods to destroy them even so, that did violate their vowed faith. [But afterwards, it would seem, when things were in such a state as constrained them to govern with a stronger hand, he bade the Athenians to **throw the perjury upon him**; and manage affairs as **convenience** required. And, in general, Theophrastus tells us] that Aristides was not only a perfect, an honest, and just man, in private matters betwixt party and party: but in matters of state, and concerning the commonwealth, he did many things oftentimes according to the necessity of the time, and troubles of the city, wherein violence and injustice was to be used. As when the question was asked in open council, to know whether they might take away the gold and silver that was left in the isle of Delos, safely laid up in the temple of Apollo, to bear out the charges of the wars against the barbarous people, and to bring it from thence unto Athens, upon the motion of the Samians (although it was directly against the articles of the alliance, made and sworn among all the Greeks). Aristides' opinion being asked in the same, he answered: "It was not just, but yet profitable."

Narration and Discussion

Themistocles and Aristides had different opinions about the skills and character qualities most required in a general. Make a list of the qualities a leader should have; choose the three you believe are the most important, and explain why you chose them. If possible, compare your list with that of someone else.

For older students: Aristides never stopped saying that he valued justice, honesty, and gentle means of negotiation. The historian quoted by Plutarch, however, said that, in practice, Aristides sometimes allowed violent and unjust actions, if the outcome seemed to be for the good of his people. Is acting against one's own conscience necessary or beneficial for a leader?

Lesson Twelve and Examination Questions

Introduction

This lesson sums up Aristides' philosophy and contributions during his lifetime; and ends with various writers' speculation about his death.

Vocabulary

capital cause: serious crime

indicted: charged

trow: think, believe

insolent: proud and rebellious

burdened: accused

minas, lugera: units of money

haven of Phalerus: Bay of Phalerum, a port of ancient Athens

Historic Occasions

471 B.C.: Themistocles ostracized

470 B.C.: death of Pausanias

468 B.C.: death of Aristides

Reading

Part One

Now, notwithstanding Aristides had brought his city to rule and command many thousands of people: yet was he still poor for all that, [and always delighted as much in the glory of being poor, as in that of his trophies; as is evident from the following story.] Callias, [the] torch bearer, was his near kinsman, [and was prosecuted by his enemies in a **capital cause**, in which, after they had slightly argued the matters on which they **indicted** him, they proceeded, besides the point, to address the judges]:

> "My Lords, you all know Aristides the son of Lysimachus, and you are not ignorant also that his virtue hath made him more esteemed than any man else is, or can be, in all Greece. How think ye doth he live at home, when you see him abroad up and down the city, in a threadbare gown all too tattered? Is it not likely, **trow** ye, that he is ready to starve at home for lack of meat and relief, whom we all see quake for very cold, being so ill-arrayed and clothed? [Callias, the wealthiest of the Athenians, does nothing to relieve either him or his wife and children in their poverty, though he is his own cousin, and has made use of him in many cases, and often reaped advantage by his interest with you.]"

Callias perceiving the judges angrier with him for that than for any matter else he was accused of: he prayed Aristides might be sent for, and willed him to tell truly whether he had not offered him good round sums of money, many a time and oft, and entreated him to take it; which he ever refused, and answered him always, that he could better boast of his poverty than [he] himself could of his riches (which he said many did use ill, and few could use them well); and that it was a hard thing to find one man of a noble mind, that could away with poverty; and that such only might be ashamed of poverty who may be poor against their wills.

So Aristides confirmed he spoke to be true; and every man that was at the hearing of this matter, went wholly away with this opinion, that he had rather be poor as Aristides, than rich as Callias. This tale is written thus by Aeschines the Socratian philosopher.

[But Plato declares that, of all the great renowned men in the city of Athens, he was the only one worthy of consideration.] "For others," said he, "[such] as Themistocles, Cimon, and Pericles, have beautified the city with stately porches, and sumptuous buildings of gold and silver, and with stone of other fine superfluous devices; but Aristides was he [who] virtuously disposed himself and all his doings, to the furtherance of the state and commonwealth."

His justice and good nature appeared plainly in his doings and behaviour towards Themistocles. For though Themistocles was ever against Aristides in all things, and a continual enemy of his, and that by his means and practise he was banished from Athens: yet when Themistocles was accused of treason to the state, having divers sharp enemies against him [such] as Cimon, Alcmaeon, [and others]: Aristides sought not revenge when he had him at his advantage. For he neither spoke nor did anything against him at that time to hurt him: neither did he rejoice to see his enemy in misery, no more than if he had never envied him in his prosperity.

Part Two

And touching Aristides' death, some write he died in the realm of Pontus, being sent thither about matters of the state; and other[s] think he died an old man in the city of Athens, greatly honoured and beloved of all the citizens.

But Craterus the Macedonian writeth of his death in this sort: [After the banishment of Themistocles, he says, the people growing **insolent**, there sprung up a number of false and frivolous accusers, impeaching the best and most influential men and exposing them to the envy of the multitude, whom their good fortune and power had filled with self-conceit.] Among the rest, Aristides was condemned for extortion and ill behaviour in the commonwealth, upon one Diophantes' accusation, of the village of Amphitrope: who **burdened** him that he took money of the Ionians, to make the annual tribute cease which they paid unto Athens: and so Craterus sayeth that because Aristides was not able to pay the fine they set upon his head (which was five **minas**), he was driven to forsake Athens, and to get him into Ionia, where he died. Yet doth not Craterus bring forth any probable matter to prove this true he writeth: as [Aristides'] pleading, his sentence and condemnation, or any decree passed against him, although he used great diligence else in collecting all such matters and vouching his authors.

[*short omission*]

Moreover, Aristides' tomb is to be seen at this day upon the **haven of Phalerus**, which was set up for him at the charge of the commonwealth, as it is reported, because he died so poor a man as they found nothing in his house to bury him with. Other[s] go further, and say that his daughters were married by decree of the people, at the charge of the commonwealth, and that the city gave every one of them three thousand drachmas: and his son Lysimachus, a hundred minas of silver, and a hundred **lugera**.

[*omission about Aristides' family*]

Narration and Discussion

Aristides said of wealth that few could use it well, so he preferred to keep himself poor. Do you agree? (Consider Matthew 19:22-24.)

Plutarch quotes Plato: "For others," said he, "[such] as Themistocles, Cimon, and Pericles, have beautified the city with stately porches, and sumptuous buildings of gold and silver, and with stone of other fine superfluous devices; but Aristides was he [who] virtuously disposed himself and all his doings, to the furtherance of the state and commonwealth." How did Aristides beautify Athens in a unique way?

Examination Questions

Younger Students:

1. Choose one of these: (a) Give two stories to show that Aristides believed it was his duty to "offer his body and life to do his country service, without prospect and hope of reward," or, (b), "I am

Alexander King of Macedon, who for the good-will…I bear you have put myself in the greatest danger." When were these words used? Describe this meeting of Alexander and Aristides.

2. (Alternate) How did Aristides (a) pacify the mutiny and (b) put an end to a conspiracy of rich noblemen before the Battle of Plataea?

Older Students:

1. (a) It is said that once when a just man was commended in the theatre "all the people straight cast their eyes upon Aristides." Give two instances to explain why the audience thought at once of Aristides; OR, b) Give an account of the conversation between Aristides and Themistocles before and after the battle of Salamis.

2. For high school students: (a) Show why Plato gave Aristides praise above all the other many famous and notable men of Athens; or, (b), Show that the counsels of Aristides brought victory to the Greek armies at Plataea.

Solon

(638-558 B.C.)

Who was Solon?

Solon was an Athenian statesman, poet, and lawgiver. He is best known for reforming his city's laws and economic policies, beginning an era of political, economic and cultural growth that would culminate in the "Golden Age of Athens."

If you have a world timeline, look at the period around 600 B.C. Solon lived during the same years as Nebuchadnezzar, Assur-bani-pal, King Josiah, Jeremiah, Daniel, and even Æsop.

Who were the rulers in Athens?

The council of elders in Athens was the **Areopagus** (see **Lesson Seven**). It was made up of men who had held high public office, such as **archon**, much like the Roman Senate.

The word **archon** simply means ruler, and it could be applied to anything from the leader of a small group to the governor of a state.

The top ruler of Athens was the eponymous archon (**archon eponymos**), who was elected for a term of one year. The word is often translated "chief magistrate," but North also translates it as **mayor** or **provost**. Solon was an archon in Athens in the year 594 or possibly 592 B.C.

Three Top Terms in Solon

If you recognize these words, you're well on your way to mastering North's vocabulary. (They will not be noted in the lessons.)

1. **stay:** halt, stop

2. **strait:** strict or narrow

3. **strange, stranger:** As in previous studies, **strange** usually means "foreign," but sometimes it just means "strange." In the story about Solon, Thales, and the stranger, the word seems to mean someone unknown to Solon.

Lesson One

Introduction

Plutarch, as he often does, begins this biography by telling about Solon's family background. We quickly move on to learning more about Solon himself, both by his vocational choice and through a meeting with someone who was determined to be his friend.

At the time that Plutarch wrote, there seems to have been a belief that merchants were *not* to be respected, since he explains that the beliefs of Solon's time were different. What are the advantages of being a merchant, according to Plutarch? Why might the people of Plutarch's time and place have thought differently?

Vocabulary

beholden to others: in debt, owing something to others

solicitous for superfluities: worrying about frills (unnecessary things)

competent necessaries: the things that are needed

discourse: conversation

People

he which first built Massilia: according to legend, that is Protis (also called Euxenes). Massilia is Marseilles, in France.

Thales, Hippocrates, Plato: well-respected Greek thinkers

Anacharsis: a Scythian philosopher

Historic Occasions

638 B.C.: birth of Solon

632 B.C.: Cylon's rebellion (see **Lesson Four**)

621 B.C.: traditional date given for the Draconian laws

On the Map

If students are unfamiliar with **Athens**, take a minute to locate it on a map and perhaps look at some pictures of the city (past and present).

Reading

Part One

[omission for mature content]

[Solon, as Hermippus writes, when his father had ruined his estate in doing benefits and kindnesses to other men, though [he himself] had friends enough that were willing to contribute to his relief, [he] was ashamed to be **beholden to others**, since he was descended from a family who were accustomed to do kindnesses rather than receive them. He therefore applied himself to merchandise in his youth; though others assure us that he travelled rather to get learning and experience [than] to make money. It is certain that he was a lover of knowledge, for when he was old he would say that he:

"Each day grew older and learned something new."]

And yet [he was] no admirer of riches, esteeming as equally wealthy the man:

["Who hath both gold and silver in his hand,

Horses and mules, and acres of wheat-land,

And him whose all is decent food to eat,

Clothes to his back and shoes upon his feet,

And a young wife and child, since so 'twill be,

And no more years than will with that agree."]

[*short omission for length*]

[And it is perfectly possible for a good man and a statesman, without being **solicitous for superfluities**, to show some concern for **competent necessaries**. In his time, as Hesiod says, "Work was a shame to none"; nor was distinction made with respect to trade; but merchandise was a noble calling, which brought home the good things which the barbarous nations enjoyed, was the occasion of friendship with their kings, and a great source of experience.] So that there have been merchants which heretofore have been founders of great cities: as **he which first built Massilia**, after he had obtained the friendship of the Gauls, dwelling by the river Rhone. And they say also, that **Thales** did traffic merchandise, and that **Hippocrates** did even so; and likewise that **Plato**, travelling into Egypt, did bear the whole charges of his journey, with the gains he made of the sale of oil he carried thither.

[Solon's softness and profuseness, his popular rather than philosophical tone about pleasure in his poems, have been ascribed to his trading life; for, having suffered a thousand dangers, it was natural they should be recompensed with some gratifications and enjoyments.] Yet it appeareth by these verses, that Solon accounted himself rather in the number of the poor, than of the rich.

["Some wicked men are rich, some good are poor,

We will not change our virtue for their store:

Virtue's a thing that none can take away;

But money changes owners all the day."]

[*omission for length about Solon's philosophical leanings*]

Part Two

[It is stated that **Anacharsis** and Solon, and Solon and **Thales**, were familiarly acquainted, and some have delivered parts of their **discourse**; for, they say,] Anacharsis, being arrived at Athens, went to knock at Solon's gate, saying that he was a stranger which came of purpose to see him, and to desire his acquaintance and friendship.

Solon answered him, that it was better to seek friendship in his own country. Anacharsis replied again: "Thou then that art at home, and in thine own country, begin to show me friendship."

Then Solon wondering at his bold ready wit, entertained him very courteously: and kept him a certain time in his house, and made him very good cheer, at the selfsame time wherein he was most busy in governing the commonwealth, and making laws for the state thereof. Which when Anacharsis understood, he laughed at it, to see that Solon imagined, with written laws, to bridle men's covetousness and injustice.

"For such laws," said he, "do rightly resemble the spiders' cobwebs: because they take hold of little fleas and gnats which fall into them, but the rich and mighty will break and run through them at their will."

Solon answered him: that men do justly keep all covenants and bargains which [they] make with [one] another, because it is to the hindrance of either party to break them; and even so, he did so temper his laws that he made his citizens know it was more for their profit to obey law and justice than to break it.

Narration and Discussion

Solon became a merchant rather than accept financial help from his friends, because his family's tradition was to confer favours, not to receive them. Do you agree with his reasoning? (If you have read the *Life of Aristides*, compare Solon's attitude toward wealth and poverty with that of Aristides.)

Anacharsis was persistent in his attempt to win Solon's friendship. Why do you think Solon was initially reluctant to welcome him? Have you ever been rebuffed by someone when you tried to be friendly? Did you keep trying? What happened?

For older students: Anacharsis said that written laws could not "bridle men's covetousness and injustice." He teased Solon by saying that written laws "were like spiders' webs, and would catch, it is true, the weak and poor, but easily be broken by the mighty and rich" (Dryden's translation). What did he mean by this? Was he right?

Lesson Two

Introduction

In this lesson, the philosopher Thales played a rather nasty practical joke on Solon, to prove that close relationships should be avoided, as they bring the risk of great grief. However, Solon (and Plutarch) had opinions to the contrary.

Vocabulary

by hap: by chance

propounded: proposed

physic and potions: medications

People

Thales: Thales of Miletus, a philosopher and mathematician

Reading

Nevertheless afterwards, matters proved rather according to Anacharsis' comparison, than agreeable to the hope that Solon had conceived. Anacharsis being **by hap** one day in a common assembly of the people at Athens, said that he marvelled much why, in the consultations and meetings of the Greeks, wise men **propounded** matters, and fools did decide them.

It is said moreover, that Solon was sometime in the city of Miletum at **Thales'** house, where he said that he could not but marvel at Thales, that he would never marry to have children. Thales gave him never a word at that present: but within [a] few days after [Thales procured a stranger to pretend that] he came but newly home from Athens, departing from thence but ten days before. Solon asked him immediately, "What news there?"

This stranger, [according to his instructions], answered: "None other there, saving that they carried a young man to burial, whom all the city followed, for that he was one of the greatest men's sons of the city, and the honestest man withal, who at that present was out of the country, and had been a long time (as they said) abroad."

"O poor unfortunate father," then said Solon, "and what was his name?"

"I have heard him named," said the stranger, "but I have forgotten him now: saving that they all said he was a worthy wise man."

So Solon, still trembling more and more for fear at every answer of this stranger; in the end he could hold no longer, being full of trouble, but told his name himself unto the stranger, and asked him again if [it] were not the son of Solon which was buried.

"The very same," said the stranger. Solon, with that, like a madman straight began to beat his head, and to say and do like men impatient in affliction and overcome with sorrow. [But Thales took his hand, and, with a smile, said, "These things, Solon, keep me from marriage and rearing children, which are too great for even your constancy to support; however, be not concerned at the report, for it is a fiction."]

Hermippus writeth that Patsecus (he which said he had Aesop's soul) reciteth this story thus.

Nevertheless, it lacketh judgement, and the courage of a man also, to be afraid to get things necessary, fearing the loss of them; for by this reckoning, he should neither esteem not honour goods, nor knowledge when he hath them, for fear to lose them. For we see that virtue itself, which is the greatest and sweetest riches a man can have, decayeth ofttimes through sickness, or else by **physic and potions**. Furthermore Thales [him]self, although he was not married, was not therefore free from this fear, unless he would confess that he neither loved friends, kinsmen, nor country; howbeit Thales had an adopted son, called Cybistus, which was his sister's son.

For our soul having in it a natural inclination to love, and being born as well to love, as to feel, to reason, or understand, and to remember: having nothing of her own whereupon she might bestow that natural love, borroweth of other[s].

[*omission*]

Now we must not arm ourselves with poverty against the grief of loss of goods; neither with lack of affection against the loss of our friends: neither with want of marriage against the death of children: but we must be armed with reason against misfortunes. [*Dryden: We must not provide against the loss of wealth by poverty, or of friends by refusing all acquaintance, or of children by having none, but by morality and reason.*] Thus have we sufficiently enlarged this matter.

Narration and Discussion

Plutarch passes on this story about Solon and Thales that he found in the writings of Hermippus (a writer of plays and poems from a later time). Do you find Thales' stunt amusing or mean-spirited? What point was he trying to make?

For older students: Plutarch says that the way *not* to lose your possessions, friends, etc. (except through inevitable things like death) is reason, or as Dryden translates it, "morality and reason." How would "morality" help to keep friendships alive? How might "reason" help you hold onto possessions, or to feel less anxious about their loss?

Lesson Three

Introduction

Plutarch, writing long after the lives of his subjects, often had the problem of trying to fit several accounts of an event into one reasonable story. Sometimes he simply gave up and presented two different versions, as here with the story of how the Athenians captured the island of Salamis. Did they really trick the Megarians by getting young soldiers to dress up like girls on the beach? Or did they capture a Megarian ship and use it to fight against the islanders? Either way, Solon led the Athenians to success.

Vocabulary

no man should presume to [propose] any more…: The Athenians forbade any further discussion about the matter

wished for somebody to begin: wished that someone would do something to regain Salamis

counterfeited a distraction: created a deception

elegiac: a formal type of verse, usually recited at *symposia* (banquets where intellectual discussion took place)

ex tempore: without formal preparation; "off the cuff"

with a cap upon his head: a cap may have been part of Solon's "herald" costume, or it may have been meant to show illness

incontinently: without any restraint

feign himself: pretend he was

straight: right away

oracle from Delphi: prophecy

bear greatest authority…: receive high positions as their reward

divers: several

in hurly-burly: in a panic

descry: figure out

securing: capturing

People

Peisistratos: also spelled Peisistratus. He was a tyrant ruler of Athens from 546 to 527/8 B.C.

Asopia, Asopus, Cychreus, Salamis: All of these names come from Greek mythology. Cychreus was the son of Poseidon (god of the sea) and Salamis, who was the daughter of the river god Asopus.

Historic Occasions

ca. 595 B.C.: The Athenian seizure of Salamis from the Megarians

On the Map

Megarians: The people of Megara, a port city in Greece, in the northern section of the Isthmus of Corinth, opposite Salamis.

Salamis: A large island that was then occupied by the Megarians.

Colias: A strip of land (promontory) on the western side of **Attica** (the territory around Athens)

Reading

Part One

The Athenians having now sustained a long and troublesome war against the Megarians, for the possession of the **Isle of Salamis**, were in the end weary of it, and made [a law] upon pain of death, that **no man should presume to [propose] any more, to the council of the**

city, the title or question of the possession of the isle of Salamis.

[Solon, vexed at the disgrace, and perceiving [that] thousands of the youth **wished for somebody to begin**, but did not dare to stir first for fear of the law, **counterfeited a distraction**; and by his own family it was spread about the city that he was mad. He then secretly composed some **elegiac** verses, and getting them by heart, that it might seem **ex tempore**, ran out into the marketplace **with a cap upon his head**. The people gathering about him, [he] got upon the herald's stand, and sang that elegy which begins thus:

"I am a herald come from Salamis the fair,

My news from thence my verses shall declare."]

This elegy is entitled "Salamis," and [it] containeth a hundred verses, which are excellently well written. And these being sung openly by Solon at that time, his friends **incontinently** praised them beyond measure, and [e]specially **Peisistratos**; and they went about persuading the people that were present to credit that [which] he spoke. Hereupon the matter was so handled amongst them, that, by and by, the proclamation was revoked, and they began to follow the wars with greater fury than before, appointing Solon to be general in the same.

Part Two

[The popular tale] is that he went by sea, with Peisistratos, unto Colias, where he found all the women at a solemn feast and sacrifice, which they made of custom to the goddess [Ceres]. He, taking occasion thereby, sent from thence a trusty man of his own unto the Megarians, which then had Salamis; whom he instructed to **feign himself** a revolted traitor, and [say] that he came of purpose to tell them that if they would but go with him, they might take all the chief ladies and gentlewomen of Athens on a sudden.

The Megarians easily believed him; and shipped forthwith certain soldiers to go with him. But when Solon perceived the ship under sail coming from Salamis, he commanded the women to depart, and instead of them he put [some beardless youths] into their apparel, and gave them little short daggers to convey under their clothes, commanding them to play and dance together upon the seaside, until their enemies were landed, and their ship at anchor; and so it came to pass. For the Megarians being deceived by that [which] they saw afar off, as soon as ever they came to the shoreside, did land in heaps, one in another's neck, even for greediness to take these women; but not a man of them escaped, for they were slain, every mother's son.

This stratagem being finely handled, and to good effect, the Athenians took sea **straight**, and coasted over to the Isle of Salamis: which they took upon the sudden, and won it without much resistance.

Part Three

Other[s] say that [Salamis] was not taken after this sort: but that [Solon first received this **oracle from Delphi**:

> Those heroes that in fair Asopia rest,
>
> All buried with their faces to the west,
>
> Go and appease with offerings of the best.]

By order of this oracle, he one night passed over to Salamis, and did sacrifice to [the heroes] Periphemus and Cychreus. [When this was] done, the Athenians delivered him five hundred men, who willingly offered themselves; and the city made an accord with them, that if they took the Isle of Salamis, they should **bear greatest authority in the commonwealth**. Solon embarked his soldiers into **divers** fishing boats and appointed a galley of thirty oars to come after him. [They anchored in a bay of Salamis that looks towards Nisaea].

The Megarians which were within Salamis, having by chance heard some inkling of it, but yet [knowing] nothing of certainty, ran presently **in hurly-burly** to arm them[selves], and manned out a ship to **descry** what it was. [This ship Solon took, and, **securing** the Megarians, manned it with Athenians, and gave them orders to sail to the island] and to keep themselves as close out of sight as could be. And he himself, with all the rest of his soldiers, landed presently, and marched to encounter with the Megarians, which were come out into the field. Now whilst they were fighting together, Solon's men, whom he had sent in the Megarians' ship, entered the [harbor] and won the town.

[omission for length: the feud between the Megarians and the Athenians was at length judged by a panel of Spartan arbitrators, in favour of the Athenians.]

Narration and Discussion

How did Solon convince the Athenians to try to do something difficult, after they were so discouraged that they refused to even listen to discussion about it? How do you think he was able to convince the Athenians (after his performance) that he was sane enough to lead the campaign? (Or did they understand all along that it was just a way to get around the law?)

For older students: Solon chose a form of poetry that was usually reserved for gatherings with a select group of well-educated men. Why did he not follow the custom and deliver the verses at a *symposium*?

Lesson Four

Introduction

This story begins with a flashback to events which happened when Solon was about six years old, involving a noble named Cylon. He led an attempt to take over the government, but the coup was unsuccessful, and the conspirators had to run for safety to the temple of Athena/Minerva. They were persuaded to come out and stand trial, but, as a symbol of Athena's protection, they unwound a rope or thread from her statue in the temple and held it as they walked to the place of trial. Unfortunately, the thread snapped, which was thought to show Athena's displeasure with the conspirators. Cylon was killed in the riot that followed; others were banished.

We also hear more about the terrible economic state in Athens. It had become common for people to use themselves as collateral for loans, meaning that if they could not pay back the money they owed, they and their families would be sold into slavery. Solon, as chief magistrate, was asked to deal with this problem.

Vocabulary

polluted: those who took part in the conspiracy

democracy: rule by "the people," meaning an assembly of citizens

oligarchy: rule by the nobles

prevailing: holding power, getting their own way

faction (1): gap

usury: lending money at unreasonably high interest rates. **Usurers** are those who lend money under such conditions.

upon gage of their bodies: using themselves as collateral, i.e. enslaving themselves to pay back debts

lustiest and stoutest: most energetic, strongest

made suit to him: asked him for help

broils: uprisings

sedition: an attempt to overthrow the government

factions (2): groups, parties

People

Cylon: also spelled Kylon or Kulon. See notes in the introduction to this lesson.

Megacles the archon: One of the principal magistrates of Athens

Epimenides of Crete: Another of the "sages"

Historic Occasions

594 or possibly 592 B.C.: Solon was archon in Athens

Reading

Part One

[omission for length: details of Cylon's rebellion, an event which caused bitter

division among the Athenians even years later]

[The Athenians, now the Cylonian sedition was over and the **polluted** gone into banishment, fell into their old quarrels about the government, there being as many different parties as there were diversities in the country. The "Hill quarter" favoured democracy; the "Plain," **oligarchy**; and those that lived by the "Seaside" stood for a mixed sort of government, and so [they] hindered either of the other parties from **prevailing**.]

Furthermore, the **faction** between the poor and rich, proceeding of their inequality, was at that time very great. By reason whereof the city was in great danger, and it seemed there was no way to pacify or take up these controversies, unless some tyrant happened to rise, that would take upon him to rule the whole.

For all the common people were so sore indebted to the rich, that either they plowed their lands, and yielded them the sixth part of their crop [*brief omission*]; or else they borrowed money of them at **usury**, **upon gage of their bodies** to serve it out. And if they were not able to pay them, then were they, by the law, delivered to their creditors, who kept them as bondmen and slaves in their houses, or else they sent them into strange countries to be sold; and many even for very poverty were forced to sell their own children (for there was no law to forbid the contrary); or else to forsake their city and country, for the extreme cruelty and hard dealing of these abominable **usurers**, their creditors. [Therefore] many of the **lustiest and stoutest** of them banded together in companies and encouraged one another not to suffer and bear any longer such extremity, but to [choose a leader, to liberate the condemned debtors, divide the land, and change the government.]

Then the wisest men of the city [perceiving Solon was of all men the only one not implicated in the troubles], neither partner with the rich in their oppression, neither partaker with the poor in their necessity; [they] **made suit to him**, that it would please him to take the matter in hand, and to appease and pacify all these **broils** and [this] **sedition**. Phanias of Lesbos writeth, that [Solon put a trick upon both parties]. He secretly promised the poor to divide the lands again; and the rich also, to confirm their covenants and bargains. [Solon, however, himself says that it was reluctantly at first that he engaged in state affairs, being afraid of the pride of one party and the greediness of the other. He was chosen archon, however, after Philombrotus, and empowered to be an arbitrator and lawgiver; the rich consenting because he was wealthy, the poor because he was honest.]

They say, moreover, that one word and sentence which he spoke (which at that present was rife in every man's mouth) [was] that equality did breed no strife [Dryden: *when things are even there can never be war*]. This did as well please the rich and wealthy, as the poor and needy. For the one sort conceived of this word "equality," that he would measure all things according to the quality of the man: and the other [group] took it for their purpose, that he would measure things by the number, and by the poll only.

Thus the captains of both **factions** persuaded and prayed him [to] boldly take upon him that sovereign authority, since he had the whole city now at his commandment. The [common people] also of every part, when they saw it very hard to pacify these things with law and reason, were [willing to have one wise and just man set over the affairs].

Part Two

[*omission: Solon refused to become sole ruler of Athens, for reasons explained in the following passage*]

But his familiar friends above all rebuked him, saying he was to be accounted no better than a beast, if for fear of the name of tyrant, he would refuse to take upon him a kingdom; which is the most just and honourable state, if one [should] take it upon him that is an honest man. [*brief omission*] He replied to his friends that it was true a tyranny was a very fair spot, but it had no way down from it. And in a copy of verses to Phocus he writes:

"that I spared my land,

And withheld from usurpation and from violence
my hand,

And forbore to fix a stain and a disgrace on my good
name,

I regret not; I believe that it will be my chiefest
fame."]

[omission for length]

Now, notwithstanding he had refused the kingdom, yet he waxed nothing the more remiss nor soft therefore in governing; neither would he bow for fear of the great, nor yet would frame his laws to their liking, that had chosen him their reformer. For where the mischief was tolerable, he did not straight pluck it up by the roots: neither did he so change the state, as he might have done, lest if he should have attempted to turn upside-down the whole government, he might afterwards have been never able to settle and [e]stablish the same again. Therefore he only altered that which he thought [he could effect by persuasion upon the pliable, and by force upon the stubborn; [and] this he did, as he himself says:

"With force and justice working both in one."

And therefore, when he was afterwards asked if he had left the Athenians the best laws that could be given, he replied, "The best they could receive."

Narration and Discussion

Solon did not want to be the king of Athens, but he was willing to be its law-giver, especially because there was so much turmoil in the city. How did he avoid coming into the situation like a bulldozer? Is this generally a good strategy for change?

What did he mean when he said he gave the Athenians "the best [laws] they could receive?"

For older students: In the poem, Solon said that he would be doing his city a favour by not having to be its harsh master, or at least to be the one responsible for having to make hard or unpopular decisions. If that is the reality of being in power, why do so many people seek it out? (Consider James 3:1; Proverbs 31:3-5.) Choose a ruler from history or literature who faced difficult decisions; and write a response to Solon from that person.

Lesson Five

Introduction

Solon had an immediate solution for the economic troubles in Athens: amnesty (forgiveness) for all debts. Everyone would start fresh. And there would be no more using people as collateral.

Did everyone like this? No; many creditors lost the money that they were owed. Some of the poor people were disappointed that Solon wasn't planning to redistribute property as well. And Solon himself came under suspicion when his friends did a bit of "insider trading."

Vocabulary

usury: see previous lesson

thwarted: stopped him from doing something

certain of his familiars: some of his friends

laid it out: spent it

their bonds: what they had owing to them

a popular state: a state under democratic rule (rather than the rule of a tyrant who could bring in new policies whenever he liked)

his ordinance: the ruling he had made

indifferently: without discriminating or leaving anything out

People

Lycurgus: (ca.800 B.C.-ca.730 B.C.) The legendary lawgiver of Sparta, who established the military-style reformation of Spartan society.

Reading

[omission for length]

The first change and reformation [Solon] made in government was this: he ordained that all manner of debts past should be clear[ed], and nobody should ask his debtor anything for the time past.

[He also ruled] that no man should thenceforth lend money out to **usury**, upon covenants for the body to be bound if it were not repaid. [Though some, [such] as Androtion, affirm that the debts were not cancelled, but the interest only lessened, which sufficiently pleased the people; so that they named this benefit the *Seisacthea*, together with the enlarging [of] their measures, and raising the value of their money. For he made a pound, which before passed for seventy-three drachmas, go for a hundred; so that, though the number of pieces in the payment was equal, the value was less; which proved a considerable benefit to those that were to discharge great debts, and no loss to the creditors. But most agree that it was the taking off the debts that was called *Seisacthea*.]

[*omission*]

But while he was a-doing this, men say a thing **thwarted** him that troubled him marvellously. For having framed an edict for clearing all debts, and lacking only a little to grace it with words and to give it some pretty preface, that otherwise was ready to be proclaimed: he opened himself somewhat to **certain of his familiars** whom he trusted (as Conon, Clinias, and Hipponicus); and told them how he would not meddle with lands and possessions, but would only clear and cut off all manner of debts. These men, *before* the proclamation came out, went presently to the money men, and borrowed great sums of money of them, and **laid it out** [immediately] upon land. So when the proclamation came out, they kept the lands they had purchased; but restored not the money they had borrowed.

This foul [act] of theirs made Solon very ill-spoken of, and wrongfully blamed: as if he had not only [allowed] it but had been partaker of this wrong and injustice. Notwithstanding, he cleared himself of this slanderous report, losing five talents by his own law. For it was well known that so much was due unto him, and he was the first that, following his own proclamation, did clearly release his debtors of the same.

[short omission]

This law neither liked the one nor the other sort. For it greatly offended the rich, for cancelling **their bonds**; and it much more misliked the poor, because [the land was not divided, and, as **Lycurgus** ordered in his commonwealth, all men reduced to equality. Lycurgus, it is true, being the eleventh from Hercules, and having reigned many years in Lacedaemon, had got a good reputation and friends and power, which he could use in modelling his state; and applying force more than persuasion, insomuch that he lost his eye in the scuffle, was able to employ the most effectual means for the safety and harmony of a state, by not permitting any to be poor or rich in his commonwealth.] Solon could not attain to this, for he was born in **a popular state**, and a man but of mean wealth. [Yet he acted fully up to the height of his power, having nothing but the good will and good opinion of his citizens to act on; and that he offended the most part, who looked for another result, he declares in the words:

"Formerly they boasted of me vainly; with averted
eyes

Now they look askance upon me; friends no more,
but enemies."

And yet had any other man, he says, received the same power:

"He would not have forborne, nor let alone,

But made the fattest of the milk his own."]

But shortly after, having a feeling of the benefit of **his ordinance**, and everyone forgetting his private quarrel: they all together made a common sacrifice, which they called the "sacrifice of *Seisachthia*"; and chose Solon general reformer of the law, and of the whole state of the commonwealth, without limiting his power, but referred all matters **indifferently** to his will. [*These were such*] as the offices of state, the common assemblies, voices in election, judgements in justice, and the body of the Senate; [and [*the power*] to dissolve or continue any of the present constitutions, according to his pleasure].

Narration and Discussion

Solon solved the problem of debtors and slavery by declaring that all previous debts were cancelled. How would you feel about that if you had lent out a lot of money? How would you feel about it if you owed a great deal? Do you think it was a wise decision overall?

How did Solon's friends take advantage of what they knew was about to happen? Why was that an embarrassment for Solon? How did he try to save face with the people?

Creative narration: Solon believed that he had offended or at least displeased many people by his proclamation forgiving debts (and forbidding extreme promises when borrowing). However, Plutarch quickly moves on to say that the Athenians "laid by their grudges" (Dryden) and began to trust Solon, asking him to make laws on other matters. Write or act out a scene showing what might have happened to shift their attitudes.

Lesson Six

Introduction

Have you ever heard of **Draco**? He lived in the seventh century B.C. and is believed to be the first lawgiver of Athens. His system of punishments was so harsh that it gave us our word "draconian."

When Solon became a lawmaker, he tried to reform some of Draco's laws to make them more reasonable and humane, and to correct some of the abuses that had come into practice. Some of his laws may sound rather picky or odd: for instance, it became illegal to export figs, and large dowries (bride prices) were outlawed. However, many of the laws were based on good reasoning.

Vocabulary

saving: except for

manslaughter: killing someone unintentionally

happily: aptly, truly

men of revenue: people with a good income

knights: the class of citizens who could afford horses, and who therefore would make up the cavalry troops in time of war. Those above them in wealth and status would be the generals, and those just below, who could afford armour and proper weapons but not horses, would be foot soldiers. Those on the very bottom rung might be rowers on a ship, or just fight with whatever they had.

it was to great purpose: Dryden says that the lowest class later found it "an enormous privilege" to be able to act as jurors

suffered: allowed

cases which he assigned…: difficult cases which had a special hearing before a judge

the letter: exactly what was written in the book

meet: proper

People

Draco: see introduction to this lesson

Aristides: see the study notes for the *Life of Aristides*

Reading

Part One

To begin withal, he first took away all **Draco's** bloody laws (**saving** [*those for*] murder, and **manslaughter**), which were too severe and cruel. For almost (Draco) did ordain but one kind of punishment, for all kind[s] of faults and offences, which was death. So that they which were condemned for idleness were judged to die; [and those that stole a cabbage or an apple were] as severely punished as those who had committed sacrilege or murder. [So that Demades, in after time, was thought to have said very **happily**], that Draco's laws were not written with ink, but with blood. And Draco himself being asked one day why his punishments were so unequal, as death for all kinds of faults: he answered, because he thought the least offence worthy [of] so much punishment: and for the greatest, he found none more grievous.

Part Two

Then Solon being desirous to have the chief offices of the city to remain in rich men's hands, as already they did; and yet to mingle the authority of government in such sort as the meaner people might bear a little sway, which they never could before; he made an estimate of the goods of every private citizen. And those which he found yearly worth [five hundred measures of fruit, dry and liquid, he placed in the first rank, calling them *Pentacosiomedimni*], as to say, **men of revenue**. And those that had three hundred bushels a year, and were able to keep a horse of service, he put in the second degree, and called them [*Hippada Teluntes*] or **knights**. [Those that had] but two hundred bushels a year were put in the third place and called *Zeugitae*. All other[s] under those, were called *Thetes*, [who were not admitted to any office, but could come to the assembly and act as jurors].

This at the first seemed nothing, but afterwards they felt it was **to great purpose**: for hereby the most part of private quarrels and strifes that grew among them were in the end laid open before the people. For he **suffered** those to appeal unto the people which thought they had wrong judgement in their causes. [Even in the **cases which he assigned to the archon's cognizance**, he allowed an appeal to the courts. Besides, it is said that he was obscure and ambiguous in the wording of his laws, on purpose to increase the honour of his courts; for since their differences could not be adjusted by **the letter**, they would have to bring all their causes to the judges, who thus were in a manner masters of the laws.]

[*omission: Solon explained his judicial policy in verse*]

Part Three

Yet considering it was **meet** to provide for the poverty of the common sort of people: he suffered any man that would to take upon him the defense of any poor man's case that had the wrong. For if a man were hurt, beaten, forced, or otherwise wronged, any other man that would might lawfully sue the offender, and prosecute law against him. And this was a wise law ordained of him, to accustom his citizens to be sorry one for another's hurt, and so to feel it, as if any part of his own body had been injured.

And they say he [once] made an answer agreeable to this law. For, being asked what city he thought best governed, he answered, "That city where such as receive no wrong do as earnestly defend wrong offered to [an]other, as [if] the very wrong and injury had been done unto themselves."

Narration and Discussion

Was it fair to grant people civil rights according to their wealth? How might such a system have caused problems for someone like **Aristides**, who said that he preferred to be poor?

Why did Solon feel it was wise to allow the laws of Athens to be slightly unclear? Who benefited from that? Would you prefer to live or work in a system with many absolute rules; or one with fewer or more flexible rules, where you are expected to make more decisions for yourself?

For older students: Solon's system of prosecution for crimes said that if I hurt someone, someone else (rather than the injured person) could take me to court over it. Can you think of reasons why this might or might not be a good idea? Would it work as a rule, say, in a classroom?

Lesson Seven

Introduction

If you could create one new law, what would it be?

Solon was given free rein to write new laws for the city of Athens, and (despite his earlier reluctance to rule), he did so quite extensively.

Vocabulary

> **Areopagus, council of the Areopagites:** As explained in the text, a high council made up of former **archons**.
>
> **imperious:** this can mean acting in a haughty and arrogant manner; but it can also mean taking on powers that you should not have
>
> **settled and stayed:** as Plutarch says, anchored; steadied, fixed in place
>
> **table(s) of Solon:** the written form of the law. The tables (or charts) were fixed in wooden frames and publicly posted (see **Lesson Nine**).
>
> **politic:** sensible, prudent
>
> **the perpetuity of discord:** the continuance of quarrels
>
> **to the public:** into the public treasury (as a fine)
>
> **amendment:** improvement
>
> **prefer:** propose, allow

Reading

Part One

[When Solon had constituted the **Areopagus** of those who had been yearly archons, of which he himself was a member therefore; observing that the people, now free from their debts, were unsettled and

imperious, he formed another council of four hundred, a hundred out of each of the four tribes, which was to inspect all matters before they were propounded by the people; and to take care that nothing but what had been first examined should be brought before the general assembly.] Moreover, he ordained the higher court should have the chief authority and power over all things, and chiefly to see the law executed and maintained, supposing that the commonwealth being **settled and stayed** with these two courts (as with two strong anchor-holds), it should be the less turmoiled and troubled, and the people also better pacified and quieted.

The most part of writers hold this opinion, that it was Solon which erected the **council of the Areopagites**, as we have said, and it is very likely to be true, for that Draco in all his laws and ordinances made no manner of mention of the Areopagites, but always speaketh to the Ephetes (which were judges of life and death) when he spoke of murder, or of any man's death. Notwithstanding, the eighth law of the thirteenth **table of Solon** sayeth thus, in these very words:

> ["Whoever before Solon's archonship were
> disfranchised, let them be restored; except those
> that, being condemned by the Areopagus, Ephetae,
> or in the Prytaneum by the kings, for homicide,
> murder, or designs against the government, were in
> banishment when this law was made."]

These words, to the contrary, seem to prove and testify that the council of the Areopagites was [in place], before Solon was chosen reformer of the laws. For how could offenders and wicked men be condemned "by order of the council of the Areopagites before Solon," if Solon was the first that gave it authority to judge? [Unless, which is probable, there is some ellipsis, or want of precision in the language, and it should run this: "Those that are convicted of such offences as belong to the cognizance of the Areopagites, Ephetae, or the Pryanes, when this law was made" shall remain still in disgrace, whilst others are restored; of this the reader must judge.]

Part Two

[*omissions for length and mature content: laws about those who did not help defend their city during rebellions, and laws designed to protect wealthy women from "gold-digging" men. Solon also made laws limiting the size of dowries (money paid by the bride's family), saying that people should marry for "pure love, kind affection, and birth of children."]*

[Another commendable law of Solon's is that which forbids men to speak evil of the dead; for it is pious to think the deceased sacred; and just, not to meddle with those that are gone; and **politic**, to prevent **the perpetuity of discord**. He likewise forbade them to speak evil of the living in the temples, the courts of justice, the public offices, or at the games; or else to pay three drachmas to the person and two to the public. For never to be able to control passion shows a weak nature and ill-breeding; and always to moderate it is very hard, and to some impossible. And laws must look to possibilities, if the maker designs to punish few in order to their **amendment**, and not many to no purpose.]

So was he marvellously well thought of for the law that he made touching wills and testaments. For before, men might not lawfully make their heirs whom they would, but [all the wealth and estate of the deceased belonged to his family]. But he, [by] leaving it at liberty [for men] to dispose their goods where they thought good, [if] they had no children of their own, did therein **prefer** friendship before kindred, and goodwill and favour before necessity and constraint, and so made everyone lord and master of his own goods.

[omission: laws forbidding exaggerated and costly mourning rituals at funerals, including the sacrifice of an ox at a graveside]

Narration and Discussion

How would you describe the laws given in this lesson? Are they reasonable? Practical?

Why did Solon say that it was just as bad to speak evil of the living as of the dead (at least in a public place)? How was this law realistic?

For older students: Discuss this saying: "And laws must look to possibilities, if the maker designs to punish few in order to their

amendment, and not many to no purpose." To what might the "possibilities" refer?

Creative narration: Write or act out a scene involving one of Solon's new laws.

Lesson Eight

Introduction

Athens was getting crowded, and there were too many people with too little to do; so Solon tried to find ways to keep everyone busy that would also build up the community.

Vocabulary

replenish: grow

repairing thither: going there

trafficking the seas: buying and selling goods by ship

relieve a father: support him financially

bred him up to any calling: taught him any trade

country of Attica: the region around Athens

requisite: necessary

bring trades into credit: make such jobs popular and attractive

brought a he-wolf: this was due to the large numbers of animals (such as sheep and goats) that were being raised in the area

Reading

Part One

Perceiving that the city of Athens began to **replenish** daily more and more, by men's **repairing thither** from all parts, and by reason of the great assured safety and liberty that they found there; and [that most of the country was barren and unfruitful], and that men **trafficking the seas** are not wont to bring any merchandise to those which can give them nothing again in exchange: [Solon turned his citizens to trade, and made a law that no son [*should*] be obliged to **relieve a father** who had not **bred him up to any calling**.

[*omission: comparison to the rule of Lycurgus in Sparta, which emphasized military skill rather than crafts*]

But Solon, framing his laws unto things, and not things unto laws: when he saw the **country of Attica** so lean and barren, that it could hardly bring forth [*enough*] to sustain those that tilled the ground only, and therefore [*it was*] much more impossible to keep so great a multitude of idle people as were in Athens: [he] thought it very **requisite** to set up occupations, and to [**bring trades into credit**]. Therefore he ordained that the council of the Areopagites should have full power and authority to enquire how every man lived in the city, and also to punish such as they found idle people [who] did not labour.

Part Two

[*omission for mature content: laws about women which even Plutarch thought contained "many absurdities." Plutarch also notes here that the fines for breaking many of Solon's laws seemed unreasonably heavy, but that this may have been due to a desperate need to add to the city's revenue.*]

More, he ordained that they which won any of the games at Athens, should pay to the common treasury a hundred drachmas. And those that won any of the Games Olympical, five hundred drachmas.

Also he appointed that he which **brought a he-wolf** should have five drachmas; and one drachma for reward of a she-wolf.

[*brief omission*]

[Since the country has but few rivers, lakes, or large springs, and many used wells which they had dug, there was a law made that, where there was a public well within a *hippicon*, that is, four furlongs, all should draw at that; but when it was farther off, they should try and procure a well of their own; and if they had dug ten fathoms deep and could find no water, they had liberty to fetch a pitcherful of four gallons and a half in a day from their neighbour's; for he thought it prudent to make provision against want, but not to supply laziness.

He showed skill in his orders about planting]: any that would plant any kind of trees in his ground, he should set them five foot asunder one from another: but for the fig tree and olive tree specially, that they should in any case be nine foot asunder, because these two trees do spread out their branches far off, and they cannot stand near other trees, but they must needs hurt them very much. For besides that they draw away the same that doth nourish the other trees, they cast also a certain moisture and steam upon them, that is very hurtful and incommodious.

More he ordained that whosoever would dig a pit or hole in his ground, he should dig it as far off from his neighbour's pit as the pit he digged was in depth to the bottom.

And he that would set up a hive of bees in his ground, he should set them at the least three hundred feet from other hives set about him before.

And of the fruits of the earth, he was contented they should transport and sell only oil out of the realm to strangers, but no other fruit or grain. He ordained that the governor of the city should yearly proclaim open curses against those that should do to the contrary, or else he himself, making default therein, should be fined at a hundred drachmas.

[*omission about owners' responsibilities for dogs that bite*]

Narration and Discussion

"He thought it prudent to make provision against want, but not to supply laziness." Which of Solon's laws put that idea into practice?

What trades might have been common in Solon's time? What are some trades that young people can train for today?

Why was it not a good idea to dig wells just anywhere?

For older students: Some say that Solon's law that only olives could be exported might have caused people to plant more olives and less grain, so that law could have caused food shortages. Do you think that could be a possible risk? Are there any similar problems with agriculture today?

For older students: Plutarch says that Solon "framed his laws unto things, and not things unto laws." What does that mean?

Lesson Nine

Introduction

What would you do if you had written all the laws you could think of but still couldn't get a free minute to yourself? How about taking a ship to Egypt to study the legend of Atlantis? Or doing some urban planning in Cyprus? Solon wanted to get out of Athens for awhile, but he kept busy along the way.

Vocabulary

> **a hundred years:** the historian Herodotus says the laws were made for ten years rather than a hundred, which might fit better with Solon's ten-year absence from Athens

> **wind himself out of these briars:** A briar patch is made up of thorny plants; once you are caught in the briars, it is difficult to get out.

> **the Atlantic story:** the story of Atlantis. Plato wrote in one of his dialogues that Solon had heard the story in Egypt and wanted to put it into verse; but it is possible that this was only in Plato's imagination.

On the Map

Find Egypt and Cyprus on the map. How might Solon have gotten there from Athens?

Reading

[omission for length: Solon's laws about immigration to Athens]

[All Solon's laws he established for **a hundred years**; and wrote them on wooden tables or rollers, named *axons*, which might be turned round in oblong cases; some of their relics were in my time still to be seen in the *Prytaneum*, or common hall, at Athens.]

[omission for length]

Now after his laws were come abroad and proclaimed, there came some daily unto him, which either praised them, or misliked them: and prayed him either to take away, or to add some thing unto them. Many again came and asked him, how he understood some sentence of his laws: and requested him to declare his meaning, and how it should be taken. Wherefore considering how it were to no purpose to refuse to do it, [*but*] again how it would get him much envy and ill-will to yield thereunto: he determined (happen what would) to **wind himself out of these briars**, and to flee the groanings, complaints, and quarrels of his citizens. For he sayeth himself:

"Full hard it is, all minds content to have,

and specially in matters hard and grave."

So, to convey himself a while out of the way, [he bought a trading vessel, and, having leave for ten years' absence, departed, hoping that by that time his laws would have become familiar].

So went he to the seas, and the first place of his arrival was in Egypt, where he remained awhile. [*short omission*] [He spent some time in study with Psenophis of Heliopolis, and Sonchis the Saite, the most learned of all the priests; from who, as Plato says, getting knowledge of **the Atlantic story**, he put it into a poem, and proposed to bring it to the knowledge of the Greeks.]

At his departure out of Egypt he went into Cyprus, where he had great courtesy and friendship of one of the princes of that country, called Philocyprus, who was lord of a pretty little city which

Demophon (Theseus' son) caused to be built upon the river of Clarius; it was of a goodly strong situation, but in a very lean and barren country. [Solon persuaded him, since there lay a fair plain below, to remove, and build there a pleasanter and more spacious city. And he stayed himself, and assisted in gathering inhabitants, and in fitting it both for defense and convenience of living; insomuch that many flocked to Philocyprus; and the other kings imitated the design; and, therefore, to honour Solon, he called the city "Soli" which was formerly named Æpea. And Solon himself, in his Elegies, addressing Philocyprus, mentions this foundation in these words:

> Long may you live, and fill the Solian throne,
>
> Succeeded still by children of your own;
>
> And from your happy island while I sail,
>
> Let Cyprus send for me a favouring gale;
>
> May she advance, and bless your new command,
>
> Prosper your town, and send me safe to land.

Narration and Discussion

How was Solon put into the position of having to be consulted on every detail of law; and how did he get out of it? How was it that the Athenians agreed to let him go at all, since they were so dependent on his advice? Can you think of any alternative solutions?

Solon claimed to be desperate to get away from all the issues in Athens; so why did he become involved with a city-building project in Cyprus?

Lesson Ten

Introduction

There used to be an expression, "rich as Croesus." Croesus (kri-sus) was the last king of Lydia (from 560 to 547 B.C.), and was famed for his wealth.

Vocabulary

by distance of time: Some say that Solon could not have visited Croesus because the chronology doesn't line up; but Plutarch says that this story is too well-known to pass over.

gaudiness and petty ostentation: extravagance and lack of taste

happy: the definition of "**happy**" is a key to this story

felicity: happiness

mean and private: without public office or recognition, or great wealth

choler: anger

amended: improved

gibbet: gallows

abashed: disconcerted; Dryden translates it "surprised"

People

Æsop: Writer of fables (620-564 B.C.)

Croesus: see the introduction to this lesson

Cyrus: Cyrus the Great, founder of the Persian Empire

Historic Occasions

546 B.C.: Croesus captured at Sardis by the Persians

On the Map

Sardis: The capital city of the kingdom of **Lydia**

Reading

Prologue

And as for the meeting and talk betwixt [Solon] and King Croesus, I know there are [*those*] that **by distance of time** will prove it but a fable, and deviced of pleasure: but for my part I will not reject, nor condemn so famous a history received and approved by so many grave testimonies. Moreover, it is very agreeable to Solon's manners and nature, and also not unlike to his wisdom and magnanimity; [because, forsooth, it does not agree with some chronological canons, which thousands have endeavoured to regulate, and yet, to this day, could never bring their differing opinions to any agreement.]

Part One

[They say, therefore, that Solon, coming to Croesus at his request, was in the same condition as a man when first he goes to see the sea; for as he fancies every river he meets with to be the ocean]; so Solon, passing alongst Croesus' palace, and meeting by the way many of the lords of his court richly appareled, and carrying great trains of serving-men, and soldiers about them, thought ever that one of them [must] had been the king; until he was brought unto Croesus [him]self. [He] was passing richly arrayed, what for precious stones and jewels, and for rich coloured silks, laid on with curious goldsmith's work, and all to show himself to Solon in most stately, sumptuous, and magnificent manner.

[Now when Solon came before him, and seemed not at all surprised, nor gave Croesus those compliments he expected, but showed himself to all discerning eyes to be a man that despised the **gaudiness and petty ostentation** of it]; then Croesus commanded all his treasuries to be opened where his gold and silver lay; next that they should show him his rich and sumptuous wardrobes, although that needed not: for to see Croesus [him]self, it was enough to discern his nature and condition.

After he had seen all over and over; being brought again unto the presence of the King, Croesus asked him if ever he had seen any man more **happy** than himself was. Solon answered:

> "I have: and that was one Tellus, a citizen of Athens,
> who was a marvellous honest man; [who] had left
> his children behind him in good estimation, and
> well to live; and lastly, was most happy at his death,
> by dying honourably in the field, in defense of his
> country."

Croesus, hearing this answer, began to judge him a man of little wit, or of gross understanding, because he [Solon] did not think that to have store of gold and silver was the only joy and **felicity** of the world, and that he would prefer the life and death of a **mean and private** man as more happy than all the riches and power of so mighty a king.

Notwithstanding all this, Croesus yet asked him again: "What other man beside Tellus he had seen happier than himself?"

Solon answered him that he had seen:

> "Cleobis and Biton, which were both brethren, and
> loved one another singularly well, and their mother
> in such sort that upon a solemn festival day when
> she should go to the temple of Juno in her coach
> drawn with oxen; because they tarried too long ere
> they could be brought; they both willingly yoked
> themselves by the necks, and drew their mother's
> coach instead of the oxen; which marvellously
> rejoiced her, and she was thought most happy of all
> other, to have borne two such sons. Afterwards
> when [the sons] had done sacrifice to the goddess,
> and [had]made good cheer at the feast of this
> sacrifice, they went to bed; but they rose not again
> the next morning, for they were found dead,
> without suffering hurt or sorrow, after they had
> received so much glory and honour."

["What," said Croesus angrily, "and dost not thou reckon us amongst the happy men at all?"

Solon, unwilling either to flatter or exasperate him more, replied:

> "The gods, O king, have given the Greeks all other
> gifts in moderate degree; and so our wisdom, too, is
> a cheerful and a homely, not a noble and kingly
> wisdom]; which, considering how man's life is

subject to infinite changes, doth forbid us to trust or
glory in these worldly riches. For time bringeth
daily misfortunes unto man, which he never
thought of, nor looked for. But when the gods have
continued a man's good fortune to his end, then we
think that man happy and blessed, and never
before. Otherwise, if we should judge a man happy
that liveth, considering he is ever in danger of
change during life: we should be much like to him,
who judgeth him the victory beforehand, that is still
a-fighting, and may be overcome, having no surety
yet to carry it away."

After Solon had spoken these words, he departed from the king's presence, and returned back again, leaving King Croesus offended, but nothing the wiser, nor **amended**. Now Æsop that wrote the fables, being at that time in the city of Sardis, and sent for thither by the king, who entertained him very honourably: was very sorry to see that the king had given Solon no better entertainment; so by way of advice he said unto him, "O Solon, either we must not come to princes at all, or else we must seek to please and content them." But Solon, turning it to the contrary, answered him: "Either we must not come to princes, or we must needs tell them truly, and counsel them for the best."

Part Two

So Croesus made light account of Solon at that time. But after he had lost the battle against **Cyrus**, and that his city was taken, himself became prisoner, and was bound fast to a **gibbet**, over a great stack of wood, to be burnt in the sight of all the Persians, and of Cyrus his enemy: he then cried out as loud as he could, thrice together: "O Solon." Cyrus, being **abashed**, sent to ask him whether this Solon [*to whom*] he only cried upon in his extreme misery was a god or man.

[Croesus told him the whole story, saying,

"He was one of the wise men of Greece, whom I sent
for, not to be instructed, or to learn anything that I
wanted, but that he should see and be a witness of
my happiness; the loss of which was, it seems, to be
a greater evil than the enjoyment was a good.] But

now (alas) too late I know it, that the riches I possessed then were but words and opinion, all which are **but** turned now to my bitter sorrow, and to present and remediless calamity. Which the wise Greek considering then, and foreseeing afar off, by my doings at that time, the instant misery I suffer now: [he] gave me warning I should mark the end of my life, and that I should not too far presume of myself, as puffed up then with vainglory of opinion of happiness, the ground thereof being so slippery, and of so little surety."

These words [*were*] reported unto Cyrus, who was wiser than Croesus; and seeing Solon's saying confirmed by so notable an example; he did not only deliver Croesus from present peril of death, but ever after honoured him so long as he lived. Thus had Solon glory for saving the honour of one of these kings, and the life of the other, by his grave and wise counsel.

Narration and Discussion

How did Solon show courage by speaking honestly to King Croesus? Wouldn't it have been simpler, and safer, to agree that the king was indeed happy? (A Scripture to consider: 2 Timothy 4:16-17)

Do you agree with Solon's definition of happiness? Might "happy" here also be translated "fortunate," or is it closer to "blessed?"

For older students: If you have a group, consider debating the definition of "happiness." This could also be the subject of an essay.

Creative narration: Retell the story of Croesus in any interesting way you choose.

Lesson Eleven

Introduction

How well did the Athenians do at keeping Solon's laws and living peacefully while he was away?

Vocabulary

The Plain, The Seaside, The Hill-Party: the various political parties described earlier

severally: independently

practise any innovation: rebel against the current order

a matter of competition: Greek drama was often staged, in later years, as a competition with prizes

inveighed: protested

stouter: braver

People

Lycurgus: Not the ruler of Sparta, but an Athenian named Lycurgus

Megacles the son of Alcmaeon: The same Megacles who was involved in killing Cylon (**Lesson Four**)

Peisistratos: see Lesson Three

Thespis of Icaria: a famous actor

Historic Occasions

565 B.C.: Peisistratos, Athenian general, organized the Diakrioi or the "Hill Party," the "party of poor people"

561 B.C.: Peisistratos took power in Athens

Reading

Part One

[When Solon was gone, the citizens began to quarrel. **Lycurgus** headed "The Plain"; **Megacles**, the son of Alcmaeon, those of "the Seaside"; and **Peisistratos** the "Hill Party," in which were the poorest people, the Thetes, and [*the*] greatest enemies to the rich; insomuch that, though the city still used the new laws, yet all looked for and desired a change of government, hoping **severally** that the change would be better for them]; and that every of them should be better than their adversaries.

[Affairs standing thus, Solon returned, and was reverenced by all, and honoured; but his old age would not permit him to be as active, and to speak in public, as formerly; yet, by privately conferring with the heads of the factions, he endeavoured to compose the differences.]

Whereunto Peisistratos seemed to be more willing than any of the rest, for he was courteous, and marvellous fair spoken, and showed himself, besides, very good and pitiful to the poor, and temperate also to his enemies; further, if any good quality were lacking in him, he did so finely counterfeit it, that men imagined it was more in him than in those that naturally had it in them indeed. As to be a quiet man, no meddler, contented with his own, aspiring no higher, and hating those which would attempt to change the present state of the commonwealth and would **practise any innovation**. By this art and fine manner of his, he deceived the poor common people.

Howbeit Solon found him straight, and saw the mark he shot at; but yet hated him not at that time, and sought still to win him, and bring him to reason; saying oftentimes, both to himself and to others, that whoso could pluck out of his head the worm of ambition by which he aspired to be the chiefest, and could heal him of his greedy desire to rule; there could not be a man of more virtue, or a better citizen than [that person] would prove.

Part Two

[**Thespis**, at this time, beginning to act tragedies; and the thing, because it was new, taking very much with the multitude, though it was not yet made **a matter of competition**; Solon, being by nature fond of hearing and learning something new, and now, in his old age, living idly, and enjoying himself, indeed, with music and with wine, went to see Thespis [*brief omission*] act; and after the play was done, he addressed him, and asked him if he was not ashamed to tell so many lies before such a number of people; and Thespis replying that it was no harm to say or do so in play, Solon vehemently struck his staff against the ground.] "But if we commend lying in sport," (quoth he), "we shall find it afterwards in good earnest, in all our bargains and dealings."

Part Three

Shortly after, Peisistratos having wounded himself, and bloodied all his body over, caused his men to carry him in his coach into the marketplace, where he put the people in an uproar, and told them that they were his enemies that thus traitorously had handled him, for that he stood with them about the governing of the commonweal[th]; insomuch as many of them were marvellously [enraged], and mutinied by and by, crying out it was shamefully done.

Then Solon, drawing near said unto him, "O thou son of Hippocrates, thou dost ill-favouredly counterfeit the person of Homer's Ulysses: for thou hast whipped thyself to deceive thy citizens, as he did tear and scratch himself to deceive his enemies."

Notwithstanding this, the common people were still in uproar, being ready to take arms for Peisistratos: and there was a general council assembled, in the which one Ariston spoke that they should grant fifty men to carry [weapons] before Peisistratos for guard of his person. But Solon going up into the pulpit for orations, stoutly **inveighed** against it [*brief omission*]. But in the end, seeing the poor people did tumult still, taking Peisistratos' part, and that the rich fled here and there, he went his way also, saying [that] he had showed himself wiser than some, and hardier than other[s]. [Wiser than those that did not understand the design; **stouter** than those that, though they understood it, were afraid to oppose the tyranny.]

Narration and Discussion

We are told that "By this art and fine manner of his, [Peisistratos] deceived the poor common people"; but that Solon immediately caught on to what he was up to. Have you known or read of anyone else who seemed well-meaning and generous, but who was motivated by ambition for power?

Why did Solon disapprove of acting out plays? What does that say about his own character?

What was Peisistratos' purpose in saying that he had been wounded by his political enemies? Were you surprised or disappointed by the fact that people believed the story?

Lesson Twelve and Examination Questions

Introduction

Peisistratos had been granted a "few" bodyguards . . . but the "few" quickly became a whole army.

Vocabulary

nice: picky

clubmen: bodyguards

Acropolis: the place of government in Athens

harken: listen

betook himself unto his ease: retired from his duties

kept his house: stayed at home

Atlantis: see note in **Lesson Nine**

Historic Occasions

558 B.C.: death of Solon

Reading

Part One

[Now, the people, having passed the law, were not **nice** with Peisistratos about the number of his **clubmen**; but took no notice of it, though he enlisted and kept as many as he would, until he seized the **Acropolis**. When that was done, and the city in an uproar, Megacles, with all his family, at once fled; but Solon, though he was now very old, and had none to back him, yet came into the marketplace and made a speech to the citizens]; and rebuked their beastliness, and faint cowardly hearts, and encouraged them not to lose their liberty; [and likewise then spoke this memorable saying]: "Before," said he, "you might more easily have stayed this present tyranny: but now that it is already fashioned, you shall win more glory utterly to suppress it."

But for all his goodly reasons, he found no man that would **harken** to him, they were all so amazed. Wherefore he hied him home again, and took his weapons out of his house, and laid them before his gate in the midst of the street, saying: "For my part, I have done what I can possible, to help and defend the laws and liberties of my country."

So from that time he **betook himself unto his ease**, and never after dealt any more in matters of state or commonwealth. His friends did counsel him to flee: but all they could not persuade him to it. For he **kept his house**, and gave himself to make verses, in which he sore reproved the Athenians' faults, saying:

["If now you suffer, do not blame the Powers,

For they are good, and all the fault was ours,

All the strongholds you put into his hands,

And now his slaves must do what he commands."]

His friends hereupon did warn him to beware of such speeches, and to take heed what he said; lest if it came unto the tyrant's ears, he might put him to death [for it. And further, they asked him wherein he trusted, that he spoke so boldly. He answered them: "In my age."

Part Two

Howbeit Peisistratos, after he had obtained his purpose, sending for him upon his word and faith, did honour and entertain him so well, that Solon in the end became one of his council, and approved many things which he did.

For Peisistratos himself did straitly keep, and caused his friends to keep, Solon's laws. Insomuch as when he was called by process into the court of the Areopagites for a murder, even at that time when he was a tyrant; he presented himself very modestly to answer his accusation, and to purge himself thereof. But his accuser let fall the matter and followed it no further.

[*brief omission*]

But Solon having begun to write the story of [**Atlantis**] in verse (which he had learned of the wise men of the city of Sais in Egypt, and was very necessary for the Athenians) grew weary, and gave it over in midway: not for any matters or business that troubled him, as Plato said, but only for his age, and because he feared the tediousness of the work. For otherwise he had leisure enough, as appeareth by his verses where he sayeth:

"I grow old, and yet I learn still."

And in another place where he sayeth,

["But now the Powers of Beauty, Song, and Wine,

Which are most men's delights, are also mine."]

[*omission: Plutarch describes Plato's own unfinished attempt to write about Atlantis*]

Solon lived [a] long time after Peisistratos had [seized the government], as Heraclides Ponticus writeth. Howbeit Phanias Ephesian writeth, that he lived not above two years after. For Peisistratos usurped tyrannical power in the year that Comias was chief governor in Athens. And Phanias writeth that Solon died in the year that Hegestratus was governor, which was the next year after that. And where some say [that] the ashes of his body were after his death strewn abroad through the Isle of Salamis: that seemeth to be but a fable, and altogether untrue. Nevertheless, it hath been written by many notable authors, and amongst others, by Aristotle the philosopher.

Narration and Discussion

After chiding the Athenians for their willingness to give up so easily, Solon gave up on them. Was Solon justified at this point?

Why was the reaction of Peisistratos unusual? Did it surprise you?

Many of Plutarch's stories end with a funeral scene, or a death in battle. This biography is much less specific about how or when Solon died. Does that make his achievements seem any less?

Examination Questions

Younger Students:

1. Give a conversation between Solon and one of the following: Anacharsis; Thales; King Croesus.

Older Students:

1. (a), "They chose Solon general reformer of the law." Write a short account of Solon as a lawgiver. OR (b) "Thus had Solon glory, for saving the honour of one of these kings, and the life of the other." Give the whole story.

2. For high school students: Give some account of (a), Solon as "reformer of the law, and of the whole state of the commonwealth," or, (b), how Solon determined to "wind himself out of these briars" of controversy and the events that followed.

Bibliography

Plutarch's Lives of the Noble Greeks and Romans. Englished by Sir Thomas North. With an introduction by George Wyndham. First Volume. London: Dent, 1894. (Solon)

https://archive.org/details/livesenglishedb01plut

Plutarch's Lives of the Noble Greeks and Romans. Englished by Sir Thomas North. With an introduction by George Wyndham. Second Volume. London: Dent, 1894. (Paulus Aemilius, Aristides)

https://archive.org/details/livesenglishedb02plut/page/n9

Plutarch's Lives: The Translation Called Dryden's. Revised by Arthur Hugh Clough. Volume 1. Boston: Little, Brown, and Company, 1865. (Solon)

https://archive.org/details/drydensplutarchs01plut/page/n4

Plutarch's Lives: The Dryden Plutarch. Revised by Arthur Hugh Clough. Volume 2. London: J.M. Dent, 1910. (Aemilius Paulus, Aristides)

https://archive.org/details/drydensplutarchs02plut/page/n4

About the Author

Anne E. White (www.annewrites.ca) has shared her knowledge of Charlotte Mason's methods through magazine columns, online writing, and conference workshops. She is an Advisory member of AmblesideOnline and the author of *Minds More Awake: The Vision of Charlotte Mason*, as well as other books in The Plutarch Project series.

Made in the USA
Middletown, DE
08 August 2021